NEON LIGHTS IN TOKYO

---

*An insider's guide to the best places
to eat, drink and explore*

BEN GROUNDWATER

EXPLORE

NEON LIGHTS
IN TOKYO

CONTENTS

WELCOME TO TOKYO

'You're going to Tokyo again?'

I hear that question regularly from friends and family. Yes, I'm going to Tokyo. Again. The city I first visited 15 years ago. The destination I've returned to almost every year since. I'm going to Tokyo again because there's still so much more I can take from this city, so much I can learn about this city, and so much I can enjoy in this city.

Tokyo, to me, is the world's most exciting place. There are some destinations that drain you as a traveller, that leave you exhausted at the end of each day, happy but ultimately deflated. Tokyo is the opposite. Tokyo gives me energy. The sheer size of it; the sheer wonder of it. Strolling the impossibly clean streets of this booming megalopolis I feel electrified, itching to explore and discover its mystery, wonder and intrigue.

Though Tokyo retains a modicum of historic charm in certain areas, for the most part this city is hyper-modern and constantly evolving. It's also clean, safe and orderly, a place where trains are always on time, residents are always polite, and a sense of community is respected even as personal space shrinks.

Tokyo is a city of the future, though sometimes it feels like a storyteller's imagining of the future, where giant billboards scream advertising slogans from skyscraper walls, where fashion is wild, where humanity teems and technology rules, the rumble of trains and the blare of arcade parlours taking the place of anything natural and real. And yet, this is real. The future is here and now.

This is also a city of passion and of perfection. Every tiny detail here has been considered and treated with respect. Look down at your feet: the manhole covers have beautiful designs engraved on them. Look at the sky: it's amazingly free of smog or grit. It's so easy to tap into Tokyo's perfection too, regardless of what you're into. Maybe you find joy in perfect plates of food, and in service that's professional and yet always convivial. Maybe you take pleasure in a carefully poured beer, drunk to the ultimate vinyl soundtrack. You might derive happiness from beautiful objects, lovingly crafted pottery or expertly cut glass. Perhaps your idea of perfection is as simple as an excellent cup of coffee, or as complex as a work of art.

Whatever your passion, you'll find it in Tokyo, and you'll find people who have made it their lives' work to achieve perfection in that field. And that, to me, makes Tokyo unique, exciting and wonderful. And it makes me want to return again and again and again.

Ben

ABOUT TOKYO

Get a window seat on your flight into Tokyo. Peer out of the plane from a great height and take in the true enormity of one of the world's great megalopolises: it's the only way you'll ever get your head around modern Tokyo's true size.

Tokyo is a settlement that began modestly, as a small fishing village called Edo some 1000 years ago, and only started to mature into the heaving beast we now know in the last five or six centuries. Edo's main castle – a building that traditionally marks a city that has graduated to a certain significance – was only built in 1457. The city became the seat of a shogunate, an area controlled by a nobleman, in 1603. And it became known as Tokyo and elevated to the capital of Japan when Emperor Meiji moved his seat from Kyoto to the city in 1869.

By then, Tokyo had grown into one of the largest cities in the world, and it continues to expand to this day, to an almost mind-boggling degree. Modern Tokyo's true borders are difficult to define: the urban sprawl has no pause as the city becomes Kawasaki and Yokohama to the south, Saitama to the north, and Chiba to the east. All told, the greater Tokyo area is now home to almost 40 million people – that's almost twice the population of Australia, squeezed into an area the same size as Sydney. So, yeah. It's big.

Since becoming the capital of Japan, Tokyo has lived through some turbulent times, including widespread and controversial Westernisation under the rule of Emperor Meiji, the Great Kanto earthquake of 1923, which killed more than 100,000 people, and a series of terrifying bombings during World War II. The city eventually recovered, however, to lead Japan's economic boom of the 1980s, a golden period that is still recalled with great affection among Tokyoites, and is visible in so much of the city's architecture and its cultural touchstones of electronics and gaming.

The Japanese capital was, of course, affected by the COVID-19 pandemic – though, with borders closed to the world for two years and strong adherence from residents to public health orders, Tokyo was able to weather the storm in impressive fashion, and many of its best venues and tourism drawcards remain open. The city continues to move ever forward, morphing and evolving as rapidly as it always has.

It retains, too, its unique cultural institutions, the distinctly Japanese venues that make any visit to this city and this country such a pleasure. Its

ABOUT TOKYO

izakaya – traditional drinking dens that serve excellent food paired with sake or beer – continue to heave well into the night with boozy salarymen and young partygoers. Its sentos – communal bathhouses similar to onsens – still ply their trade to health-obsessed clientele across the city. Its coffee shops bustle. Its train stations heave. Its high-end restaurants tinkle and murmur. This is still, in short, a city of everything. A city that has everything. A city that is everything.

The question, therefore, is how do you sum up somewhere so enormous and so filled with every single aspect of humanity? How do you share what makes it unique, what makes it a joy and so attractive? In considering the writing of this book, I've come to realise that what sets Tokyo apart is the way so many sub-cultural niches find their natural home here, and the way its people work so hard to perfect the object of their passion, be it food or drink, art or design, sport or nature.

There's even a name for it in Japanese: kodawari, the relentless pursuit of perfection. Kodawari is a mark of respect for something good. It's serious in its recognition that there is value and honour in making sure everything is just so, in making everyone's lives just that bit more pleasurable. And the good news is that it will make your life more pleasurable, too.

And so in figuring out how to codify and quantify such a gigantic, multi-faceted place, I have decided to focus on its obsessive nature, on the ability of Tokyo's residents to focus on one small point of passion and spend a lifetime perfecting it. I love these obsessions, even if they are not always my own. I love delving into them and coming to appreciate what it is that makes people so passionate and knowledgeable about them.

To the visitor, these obsessions can be treated much like the physicality of Tokyo itself: they're vast networks both underground and over that you can dive into and explore with all the passion and vigour that you deem necessary. And when you're done, you can simply step into another. The residents of Tokyo are, by and large, welcoming and kind, willing to share their passions, or at least to allow a window for others to gaze into.

Something that should be noted, however, is that I don't propose this as a definitive list of Tokyo's best and finest. This city is just so huge, and it changes so quickly, that anyone claiming such a thing would be delusional. My aim in this book, instead, is to share a few of my favourite iterations of various venues – restaurants, cafes, shops, arcades, izakaya, temples, museums and sentos – and to arm you with the knowledge and the confidence to explore further, to know what to look for and where to look for it and to duck behind the curtain of Tokyo and see what you can find.

This is an incredible and exciting city, with a long history and an exciting future. All you have to do is look.

TOKYO

Key

1. Senso-ji
2. Tokyo Skytree
3. Imperial Palace
4. Kusunoki Masashige
5. Shibuya Scramble
6. Meiji Jingu shrine
7. Studio Ghibli Museum
8. Inokashira Park

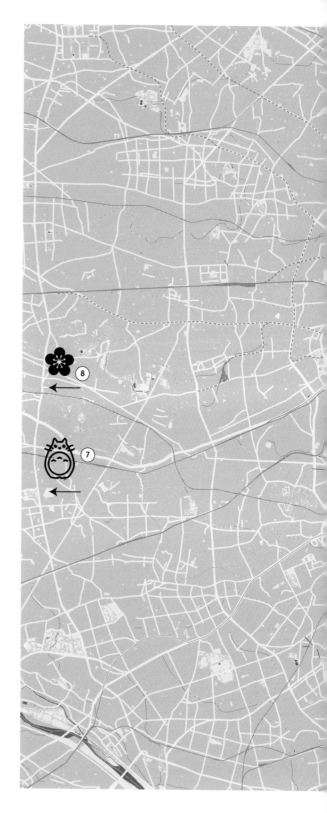

NEIGHBOURHOOD INDEX

NEIGHBOURHOOD INDEX

NOTABLE NEIGHBOURHOODS

Tokyo is a city of villages, a place that may at first seem huge and intimidating, but is actually a network of easily digestible neighbourhoods that are all connected and yet culturally distinct. These areas are known as chos – a Japanese delineation similar to a suburb – and the trick is to focus on just one or two a day, to allow time to wander and discover in each of them, to enjoy everything the city has to offer without needing to jump on a train and immediately go somewhere else.

It's easy to spot a theme to most of Tokyo's chos, to know what you'll be getting when you choose each neighbourhood as your destination. It might be nightlife, it might be vintage stores, it might be high fashion, it might be electronics. It might be something completely different. But it will always be interesting.

AKASAKA

This central Tokyo district is about as upscale as the city gets, a haven for politicians and high-flying businesspeople, a place filled with expensive restaurants – such as the lovely Eigetsu (see p.45) – and luxury hotels.

AKIHABARA

The sheen might have faded slightly from Tokyo's famed electronics town, but Akihabara is still a neighbourhood that is obsessed with technology. This is the place to come for all gadgets and machines, but it's also a hub of gaming and geek culture, with plenty of manga stores and arcade parlours in among the electronics shops.

NOTABLE NEIGHBOURHOODS

ASAKUSA

This is probably Tokyo's most historic neighbourhood, filled with Edo-era touches, and it's certainly the city's most popular with tourists – annoyingly so at times. Asakusa is mostly about temples such as Senso-ji (see p.69), shrines and traditional restaurants (as well as a slew of fairly middling tourist-focused eateries), though thanks to Kappabashi Kitchen Street (see p.57) it's also a must-visit for anyone interested in cooking.

BENTENCHO

There's little reason to visit this quiet neighbourhood in Tokyo's north other than to visit the Yayoi Kusama Museum (see p.163). It's well worth the journey.

EBISU

Ebisu is one of those perfect in-between suburbs, both geographically and culturally. Set to the south of Shibuya and the north of Nakameguro, it's a bustling hub that nevertheless has plenty of quiet corners and cosy venues like Bar Track (see p.126). Come here for nightlife designed for grown-ups.

GAKUGEI-DAIGAKU

Step off the train in Gakugei-Daigaku, in Tokyo's south-western suburbs, and it's as if you've left the city entirely: gone are the skyscrapers and the bustle, replaced by quiet, pedestrian-friendly streets and welcoming little shops and eateries. This neighbourhood is a sleeper hit, the perfect place to while away an afternoon drinking good coffee at Higuma Doughnuts (p.151), eating tasty food at Bigiya Ramen (see p.46) and taking it slow.

GINZA

Some of the world's most expensive real estate can be found in Ginza, Tokyo's downtown business district, all towering skyscrapers and wide, busy streets. Wander those streets and you will see Tokyo's largest department stores (like Mitsukoshi, see p.95), its biggest shopping malls (like Ginza Six, see p.161), and its priciest restaurants. If you have money to spend, Ginza is the place.

HARAJUKU

Flashy, fashionable Harajuku has been made world famous thanks to the 'Harajuku girls' in their cosplay outfits – who, by and large, don't go to Harajuku anymore – as well as the Gwen Stefani song of the same name. This place is maximum Tokyo, all bright lights and kawaii (cute) culture, a little tacky and a bit hectic, but an experience all the same.

NOTABLE NEIGHBOURHOODS

HIGASHI-AZABU

The Azabu area, in central Tokyo, includes Azabu-Juban, Nishi-Azabu, Azabudai, and Higashi-Azabu. All are roughly similar neighbourhoods, expensive areas that feature a blend of old-money charm and fancy new development. There are a lot of foreign embassies, and shops and restaurants that cater to the foreign crowds. Head here for excellent food at Pizza Studio Tamaki (see p.109).

IKEBUKURO

Consider Ikebukuro as the thinking traveller's Akihabara: a busy and thoroughly modern neighbourhood just to the north of Shinjuku, which has otaku (geek) and tech culture, with great tourist-free bars and places to eat.

KANDA

Kanda doesn't get much love from tourists, as it's often lost among neighbours like Nihonbashi and Ginza. There is, however, good reason to head up here, and that's to visit mAAch ecute Kanda Manseibashi (see p.54), a yokocho (narrow street) strip of designer and artisan shops under the railway tracks.

KICHIJOJI

Out in Tokyo's west, Kichijoji is like a 'Little Shibuya', an area with great nightlife, excellent food, plus big department stores and chain shops – only, everything is just a little smaller and more manageable than its more famous cousin. This is frequently voted Tokyo's most liveable area, and once you've spent a little time here eating and drinking in Harmonica Yokocho (see p.87), shopping on Nakamichi-dori (see p.169), hanging out at Inokashira Park (see p.218) and enjoying the family-friendly vibes, you will understand why.

KIYOSUMI

This traditional, residential part of eastern Tokyo has somewhat surprisingly become the home of numerous hipster coffee roasteries and cafes, as well as artisanal ramen in the form of Yuji (see p.101).

KOENJI

Like vintage? Vintage clothes, vintage shoes, vintage records? Koenji is the suburb for you. There are literally hundreds of quirky and well curated shops within easy striking distance of the train station. Koenji also has some of Tokyo's best music venues, particularly if you're into punk or experimental.

NOTABLE NEIGHBOURHOODS

KURAMAE

This is design town: the place to go for all of your art and craft supplies, and to pick up unique clothing and household items produced by local designers and artisans, particularly at the likes of M+ (see p.47) and Maito (see p.61).

MEGURO

Meguro might lack the edgy, on-trend reputation of neighbouring Nakameguro, but it still has plenty to recommend it, not least a few historic restaurants, such as Tonki (see p.83), and a laidback charm. There are plenty of parks and shrines here that offer the perfect break from the busy city.

MUSASHI-KOGANEI

Lying a half-hour train ride west of Shinjuku, Koganei isn't exactly a tourist hotspot: however, thanks to the Edo-Tokyo Open-Air Architectural Museum (see p.77), and the beauty of Koganei Park, intrepid explorers will be rewarded.

NAKAMEGURO

This is one of Tokyo's coolest chos, which has boomed in recent years with plenty of boutique shops, high-quality restaurants and excellent cafes throwing open their doors. Nakameguro also has a string of interesting museums, and its little river (see p.215) is one of Tokyo's most popular spots for sakura (cherry blossom) spotting during the spring season.

NAKANO

Just one train stop from Shinjuku, Nakano is geek heaven given its status as the home of Mandarake (see p.187), the famed network of shops stocking every collectable imaginable. Nakano also has a charming shotengai (old-school shopping street), plus a lovely temple, Araiyakushi Baishoin (see p.75).

NIHONBASHI

The name means 'Japan Bridge', and that's what this neighbourhood is famous for, that iconic, 17th-century landmark that has functioned as the kilometre-zero marker for Japan's national highway network since the Edo period. Nihonbashi these days is an upmarket commercial hub that also hosts Japan's most important sumo training centre: Arashio-beya Sumo Stable (see p.89).

NOTABLE NEIGHBOURHOODS

OGIKUBO

Another of the many pleasant, friendly villages to the west of Shinjuku, Ogikubo doesn't have the buzz of neighbours like Koenji and Kichijoji, though it does have some great old-school restaurants and bars. Head out here to eat some of Tokyo's best ramen at Harukiya (see p.85), to go antique shopping, or sake buying at Mitsuya Saketen (see p.203) in Nishi-Ogikubo.

OMOTESANDO

Few suburbs are as flashy as Omotesando, near Harajuku and Shibuya in Tokyo's inner-west. All of the big-name fashion designers are here, most in buildings that are attractions in themselves. Fortunately, looking is free.

ROPPONGI

This notorious expat haven has more than its share of dive bars and seedy nightclubs, though large-scale developments, such as the Mori Art Museum (see p.159), have brought a touch of class (and a few daytime attractions).

RYOGOKU

The home of Tokyo's sumo stadium, Ryogoku Sumo Hall (see p.89), has an old-school charm that's worth experiencing, particularly if you'll be heading to a wrestling bout at the same time. There are plenty of temples and shrines in Ryogoku, as well as a few high-end, traditional eateries.

SHIBUYA

Shibuya is the future, though it's a *Back to the Future* future, where J-pop music is piped on narrow streets, where moving billboards call out to you from skyscraper walls, where everything is new and trendy and completely bewildering. Come to Shibuya to see the famous Shibuya Scramble pedestrian crossing (see p.147). Come for the shopping. Come for the nightlife and the great izakaya (local sake bars). Come to see what the whole world could be.

SHIMOKITAZAWA

Shimokita's status as an under-the-radar hipster paradise has been eroded in recent years by the creep of gentrification: the suburb that used to be all designer boutiques and cooler-than-thou vintage stores now has a huge Muji and a Uniqlo as well. This is still, however, a stylish neighbourhood with plenty to recommend it, with narrow, pedestrianised streets, great shops and restaurants and some of Tokyo's best live music venues.

NOTABLE NEIGHBOURHOODS

SHINAGAWA

Tokyo's key southern transport hub (conveniently close to Haneda Airport, see p.221) is essentially a city in its own right, with a population nearing half a million, and one of the busiest train stations in the capital. There are plenty of major hotels in Shinagawa, as well as restaurants, shopping malls and specialty shops such as Pigment (see p.166).

SHINJUKU

More than 3.5 million people use the Shinjuku train station every day, which gives you an idea of the scale of this place. This is the home of Kabukicho, Tokyo's red-light district, as well as Golden Gai (see p.201), its best dive-bar area, plus all of the shops, restaurants and drinking holes you could imagine, packed both high above ground and well below the surface.

TOMIGAYA

Tomigaya is cool. It's far enough away from Shibuya to be boutique, though close enough to attract a crowd. If you want to see people with twirly moustaches riding fixed-gear bicycles and wearing high-end vintage fashion, then Tomigaya is your spot. This is also a great place for a decent espresso-style coffee at Coffee Supreme (see p.111) and an unusually early breakfast (for Tokyo) at Path (see p.117).

YOYOGI-UEHARA

Yoyogi provides a pleasantly quiet break from Shibuya, just nearby; it's a residential neighbourhood that sports a couple of high-quality boutiques, and restaurants such as Fuku Yakitori (see p.53).

YURAKUCHO

Nestled into a corner of Ginza, Yurakucho is a little cheaper and quieter, with Tokyo's largest concentration of 'antenna' stores, and a bustling horde of cheap izakaya (local sake bars) and yakitori joints underneath the railway line.

A NOTE ON ADDRESSES

You will quickly discover that the addresses used in this book don't look like any addresses you've ever seen before. And that's with good reason: Tokyo's system of addressing is unique. There are no street names here. Instead, you will find addresses that read like: 2-24-12 Shimomeguro, Meguro-ku. Ah ... what?

Essentially, Tokyo addresses break the city down into smaller and smaller parts. First the entire city is divided into 'wards', which is the word in the address ending in 'ku'. Then there's the 'cho', a smaller division of the ward. The cho is then further divided into several 'chome'. Each chome is then broken down into numbered blocks, and the buildings within each block are also numbered.

2-24-12 SHIMOMEGURO, MEGURO-KU

So, in the address above Meguro-ku is the ward, Shimomeguro is the cho, and the first number in the sequence, 2, is the chome. The second number, 24, is the number of the city block that the building you're looking for is placed on. And the third number, 12, is the actual building number.

If that sounds confusing, it is – especially as the buildings on a Tokyo block are sometimes numbered in the order in which they were built, rather than in a clockwise or anti-clockwise sequence around the block.

So take my advice here and don't bother looking for addresses. They're far too complicated. Instead, use a map app (see p.222), punch in the name of the shop, bar or restaurant that you're looking for, and follow the suggested route to get there. And remember that once you arrive at the right building, the venue you're looking for could be above or below you, not just in front.

Neighbourhoods

ARTS AND EDO-ERA DELIGHTS

FULL-DAY ITINERARY

Tokyo's north-eastern neighbourhood of Asakusa is something of a tourist favourite, one of the few areas that still boasts genuine Edo-era charm, with plenty of temples and gardens, restaurants and shotengai (traditional shopping streets) to explore. Asakusa also provides easy access to Kuramae, an up-and-coming district that forgoes the Edo architectural charm in favour of tradition in design, with beautiful little shops specialising in stationery, fabrics, leathergoods and more.

10AM Begin your day in the centre of Asakusa. Exit the train station at the Kaminarimon gate and walk north along Nakamise Shopping Street, ignoring the tacky tourist shops and making your way up to ① **Senso-ji** (see p.69). This temple is one of Edo-era Tokyo's most important landmarks, and worth fighting the crowds (which will hopefully be thin at this time of the morning) to explore.

11AM From Senso-ji, walk west through historic Asakusa, winding through a few quiet alleys before arriving at ② **Kama-Asa** (see p.57), a knife shop on Kappabashi Kitchen Street. This is traditionally a place for restaurateurs to buy wholesale goods, though these days there's plenty for consumers, from Japanese knives to pots and pans, crockery, chopsticks, and even the plastic models of food that you see on display in restaurants.

12PM It's now time for a wander north into the slightly sleazy neighbourhood of Minowa (keep an eye out for all the dens of ill-repute – closed at this time of day – as you walk north-east along Nakanocho-dori). Your destination is worth it: ③ **Dote no Iseya** (see p.76), a historic tempura restaurant. Queue up, take a seat, and order a huge bowl of fried seafood and vegetables atop rice.

2PM After lunch, walk off that big meal on the journey back to Asakusa, walking south-east on Dote-dori, before making a right at the third set of traffic lights and heading south-west towards ④ **Taiko-Lab** (see p.79). Here you'll be getting another workout with a drumming lesson, a crash course in beating huge taikos with large sticks – be sure to book ahead.

3PM Once the lesson is over, you have the choice of either walking south about 25 minutes into Kuramae, or calling in at Asakusa station and taking the subway instead. Regardless, you'll soon find yourself at ⑤ **Koncent** (see p.167), where you can pick up an excellent coffee while browsing the Japanese homewares. This is the craft and design portion of the walking tour, where you'll spend a good part of the afternoon exploring the quiet streets of Kuramae. Continue on to ⑥ **M+** (see p.47), a purveyor of fine handmade leather goods. Next, walk to ⑦ **Maito** (see p.61), which specialises in clothes dyed using a traditional technique. Then walk four blocks west, over to Shinbori-dori to explore the ⑧ **Mokuba Showroom** (see p.49), which is packed with high-end ribbons. Finally, continue west to ⑨ **Kakimori** (see p.168), one of Tokyo's finest stationery shops.

6PM Make your way back to Asakusa for an early dinner at ⑩ **Namiki Yabusoba** (see p.73), a restaurant that has been turning out soba noodles for more than a century. It's easy to find, too – just a 3-minute walk from Asakusa train station.

7.30PM From Namiki, walk back to Asakusa station and take the Asakusa line two stops over to Oshiage station, which provides easy access to ⑪ **Tokyo Skytree** (see p.173). Time this visit right – including by booking your tickets online in advance – and you'll be able to catch 'golden hour' from the city's best vantage point, as the sun sets and the lights of Tokyo begin to twinkle.

A NOTE ON BREAKFAST

You'll note that some of the itineraries don't include a breakfast option, because breakfast isn't much of a thing in Japan. Most people will have a light meal at home, or grab a quick snack from a train station.

THE BIG END OF TOWN
FULL-DAY ITINERARY

This is where it all happens. All the big deals. All the important meetings. All the fancy purchases. Ginza is Tokyo's 'big end of town', the central business district to end all central business districts, home to some of the most expensive real estate, restaurants and shops in the world. But spending time here needn't be budget-busting. With a mix of window-shopping, small purchases and carefully selected bars and restaurants, it's possible to soak up everything that makes Ginza amazing, while still having enough money for the train fare home.

9AM Tokyo tends to rise late, and you'll find most shops won't open until at least 10am. Still, that doesn't mean you have to hibernate. Today begins at the still quite civilised time of 9am with a wander around the ① **Imperial Palace** (see p.91) gardens before the crowds arrive. Though the primary residence of the Emperor of Japan is closed to the public, the sprawling traditional gardens are free to explore, and a wander here is the perfect way to ease into the day.

10AM Once you're finished exploring the gardens, make your way south, past the statue of Kusunoki Masashige – a famous samurai – on your left, across the moat and into Yurakucho. This neighbourhood is like a mini Ginza, with cheaper real estate and consequently some better-value shopping. Begin by taking a wander around ② **Bic Camera** (see p.164), which stocks every electronic good imaginable. Next, duck under the train lines and call into Kotsu Kaikan, an old-school shopping mall filled with Tokyo's best prefectural 'antenna' stores, like ③ **Hokkaido Dosanko Plaza** (see p.48).

11.30AM Time to make a brief foray north, taking a short walk to Yurakucho station and catching a Keihin-Tohoku line train to Akihabara station. From there, walk back across Kanda River, on Mansei Bridge, and then immediately take a right: you've arrived at ④ **mAAch ecute Kanda Manseibashi** (see p.54), a former train station turned artisan market, where you can pick up all sorts of unique, handmade goods before grabbing a coffee by the train tracks (or a craft beer at Hitachino).

1PM Next, walk south about 7 minutes to Kanda station and catch the Ginza line to Kyobashi station. Take exit 6 and walk a few metres to your lunch spot: ⑤ **Fukamachi** (see p.59), a Michelin-starred tempura joint that takes fried food to a whole new level. It's quite expensive, though lunch here is far cheaper than dinner, and represents great value to those hoping to sample some of Tokyo's best cuisine. Book well in advance for this one. For a cheaper eat, grab vegan ramen at T's TanTan (see p.113).

2PM It's time to (window) shop till you drop, with a quick tour of some of Ginza's most interesting stores. Begin by walking south-west down Ginza's main thoroughfare to ⑥ **Mitsukoshi** (see p.95), a department store that has been in business since 1673, and that boasts one of the best depachikas (basement food halls) in the city. Later, walk over to ⑦ **Yoseido Gallery** (see p.157) to browse the wood-block art prints, and then visit ⑧ **Lemon Inc** (see p.121) for all of your vintage camera and watch needs.

4PM Here's a break from the ordinary. After Lemon, take a 2-minute walk over to ⑨ **HiSUi** (see p.71), a traditional dojo where you can book ahead and take a class to learn calligraphy, kimono dressing, how to conduct a tea ceremony, or sword fighting. I would recommend the latter, particularly if you fancy the idea of slicing through a bamboo mat with a razor-sharp katana.

5PM There's time to relax after the HiSUi experience, with a 10-minute walk south to ⑩ **Café de l'Ambre** (see p.78), a traditional Tokyo kissaten. These old-style coffee shops don't always make a great brew but Café de l'Ambre is different: it has been open since 1948 and is staffed by absolute coffee masters, who grind the best beans and make a truly excellent, if pricey, brew.

6PM Full of energy after your caffeine hit, walk a block up to ⑪ **Ginza Six** (see p.161), one of the area's newest and fanciest shopping malls. With luxe residents such as Dior, Valentino, Fendi and Yves Saint Laurent this might be more an exercise in gazing than anything else but, still, this is a beautifully designed building that is a pleasure to explore for an hour or so; head to the rooftop terrace to take in views of Ginza.

7PM Time for dinner. Ginza has an embarrassment of excellent options, from Tokyo's most famous high-end sushi bars to the raucous and affordable yakitori izakaya (local sake bars) in Yurakucho. Your choice for tonight, however, falls somewhere in between: ⑫ **Ginza Shimada** (see p.198), a tachinomi (standing bar) that serves extremely high-quality, kaiseki-style (multi-course) cuisine in a relaxed environment. Dishes here are small, and meant to be paired with sake. Order one drink and one dish, rinse and repeat.

9PM You can't leave Ginza without sampling its famed cocktail culture. From Shimada, it's about a 5-minute walk through narrow streets to ⑬ **Bar Yu-Nagi** (see p.196), which specialises in cocktails using organic fruits and vegetables from around Japan.

HIGH FASHION
TO THE HIGH LIFE

FULL-DAY ITINERARY

This is the Tokyo you've been picturing: the neon jungle, the skyscrapers and bright lights, the outlandish fashion, the crowds, the good times. Harajuku and Shinjuku are justifiably famous neighbourhoods, given their status at the forefront of Tokyo's fashion and nightlife scenes, areas known as much for their boutique shopping and tiny, cosy bars as for their whopping department stores and world-famous brands. This walking tour takes in a little of everything, from high-end vintage shopping in Harajuku to the dive bars of Shinjuku, with some relaxation in between.

10AM Your day begins by taking the subway to Omote-Sando station, where you'll alight and walk 5 minutes south-east to the ① **Nezu Museum** (see p.84). This establishment houses the private art collection of Nezu Kaichiro, with more than 7000 pieces of Japanese and East Asian art.

11AM Take a slow stroll back towards Omote-Sando station, passing the area's many ② **high-end fashion outlets** (see p.175) along the way. Keep your eye out for Comme des Garçons, Stella McCartney, Prada, Issey Miyake, Miu Miu, Balenciaga, Alexander McQueen and more – all perfect for a little dreamy window-shopping.

12PM It's now lunchtime by Tokyo standards, so continue walking to ③ **Maisen** (see p.106), one of the city's premier tonkatsu (deep-fried pork) restaurants. A large hunk of fried pork and a side salad will set you up for the rest of the day. (For vegetarians, Afuri – see p.104 – does a vegan ramen, and is in nearby Harajuku.)

1PM You won't have to walk much further through the buzzing streets of Aoyama to reach ④ **Solakzade** (see p.135), an absolute treasure-trove for anyone interested in vintage eyewear. Later, stroll through the uber-cool streets of Harajuku to reach ⑤ **Toro Vintage Clothing** (see p.131), for men's and women's vintage that's extremely well curated.

2.30PM Continue your wanderings north, through the busy streets of Kita-Sando and Sendagaya, before arriving at ⑥ **Shinjuku Gyoen National Garden** (see p.216). This is one of Tokyo's best parks, a beautifully manicured space that provides ideal succour from the bustle of the city. Take your time exploring and maybe stopping for tea at the Rakuutei Tea House before exiting at the north of the park.

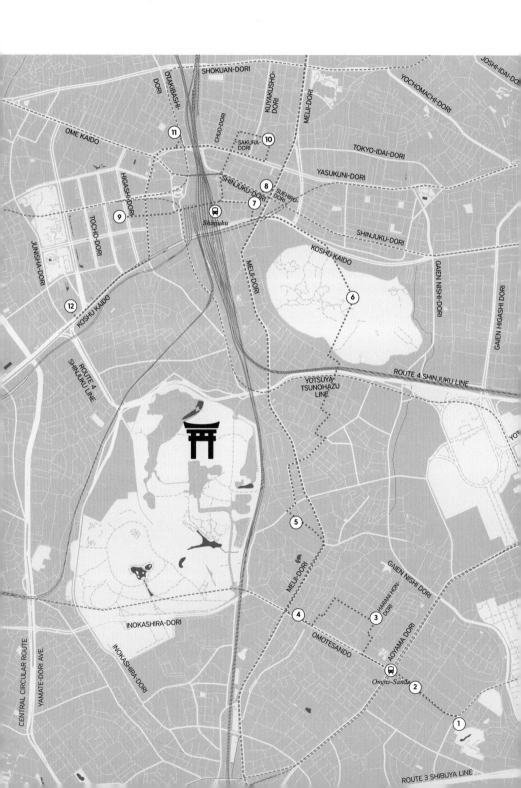

4PM A short walk to the north-west, in Shinjuku Sanchome, you'll find the vast network of ⑦ **Disk Union** (see p.123) stores. These are some of Tokyo's best purveyors of second-hand vinyl, and if you're a collector you will want to spend hours trawling. Even for those with a casual interest, however, these record stores are amazing.

5PM It's only a 2-minute walk from Disk Union to ⑧ **Isetan** (see p.103), one of Shinjuku's premier department stores, a colossal store featuring some of the best in men's and women's fashion and accessories, as well as an excellent depachika (basement food hall), if you need a late afternoon snack.

6PM From Isetan, walk west through Shinjuku train station towards Nishi-Shinjuku, where you'll find Keio Plaza, the luxury hotel that's the home of tonight's dinner venue: ⑨ **Kyubey** (see p.51). Kyubey is a high-end sushi joint, one where you'll sit at the bar and watch as a chef prepares a sumptuous feast of seafood delicacies. Ensure you book ahead and know the art of sushi before you go (see p.226).

8PM After dinner, stroll back through the station and make a left into Kabukicho, Tokyo's red-light district, and just walk around and take in the lights, billboards and the seediness. Later, walk a few blocks east to ⑩ **Golden Gai** (see p.201), where you can take a few drinks at your bar of choice.

10PM The night is still young as far as Shinjuku is concerned. From Golden Gai, walk back over to the west to call into ⑪ **Zoetrope** (see p.205), one of Tokyo's best whisky bars. Alternatively, have a nightcap at ⑫ **New York Bar** (see p.140), the ideal place from which to take in this incredible city.

HOME OF THE HIPSTERS
FULL-DAY ITINERARY

Where do Tokyo's hipsters hang out? In the west, particularly around neighbourhoods such as Tomigaya and Shimokitazawa. This itinerary takes in both of those trendy haunts, with a few other nearby suburbs thrown in – though this isn't just for the cool people. The day offers a mix of vinyl, vintage and quirky department store shopping, plus eating and drinking in a range of establishments, running on a relaxed schedule that should see you heading home with armfuls of boutique purchases and a belly full of delicious food.

9AM Begin your outing at ① **Path** (see p.117), a Tomigaya cafe with some excellent Western-style breakfast options, as well as great coffee.

10AM Just a 5-minute stroll down the road, ② **Meals are Delightful** (see p.171) stocks a wide range of beautiful ceramic tableware, the exact thing you need if you're hoping to recreate some of the food you've eaten in Tokyo back home.

11AM It's time to leave the quiet streets of Tomigaya and cross into Shibuya, where you'll find ③ **Tokyu Hands** (see p.174), an amazing department store that stocks every fascinating gadget and knick-knack you could imagine. From there, continue east to the appropriately towering ④ **Tower Records** (see p.148), where you can spend as much time as you need trawling through vinyl and CDs.

12.30PM Lunch today is just a 10-minute walk away, winding through Shibuya's busy streets to ⑤ **Kabe no Ana** (see p.92). This is Japan's original wafu pasta (Japanese style) joint, where the salmon roe and sea urchin spaghetti is highly recommended.

2PM Your next stop is – wait for it – Starbucks. Yes, ⑥ **Starbucks Shibuya** (see p.147). Not for the amazing coffee but for the amazing view of the Shibuya Scramble, the famously chaotic pedestrian crossing near the train station. Once you've grabbed a few photos and a pumpkin-spiced mocha-choca-latte, head across to the station and catch a train to Shimokitazawa.

2.30PM It's time to soak up some of Shimokita's hipster cool, first with a visit to ⑦ **Flash Disc Ranch** (see p.129), a great record store with a friendly owner. From here, take a 5-minute wander through the area's dollhouse streets (possibly calling into a few boutiques on your way) to ⑧ **Flamingo** (see p.127), one of the many vintage stores here.

4PM After the shopping spree, walk a few minutes north to ⑨ **Bear Pond Espresso** (see p.107), where you'll get one of Tokyo's best coffees, if not its friendliest welcome.

5PM You now have a choice. If you're feeling energetic you could walk about 25 minutes north-east through admittedly fairly plain streets to neighbouring Yoyogi-Uehara. Alternatively, catch the train one stop from Shimokitazawa to Yoyogi-Uehara station.

6PM Dinner tonight will be eaten at ⑩ **Fuku Yakitori** (see p.53), where simple grilled chicken is elevated to levels you wouldn't believe. The restaurant takes bookings, but if you arrive early – at around 6pm – there's also the chance of nabbing a table as a walk-in.

8PM You haven't done Tokyo's trendy inner-west until you've been to a natural wine bar, and ⑪ **Ahiru Store** (see p.207) is the best of them. This is only a 15-minute walk from Fuku Yakitori, making it a perfect journey to work off the food and work up a thirst for Ahiru's impressive selection of predominantly French natural wines.

9PM Still have some stamina? If you don't get too comfortable at Ahiru, it's worth jumping on the train back to Shimokitazawa to catch a live show at ⑫ **Shelter** (see p.141), a legendary music venue in a small basement. Tickets are sold on the door, and the music trends hard and loud.

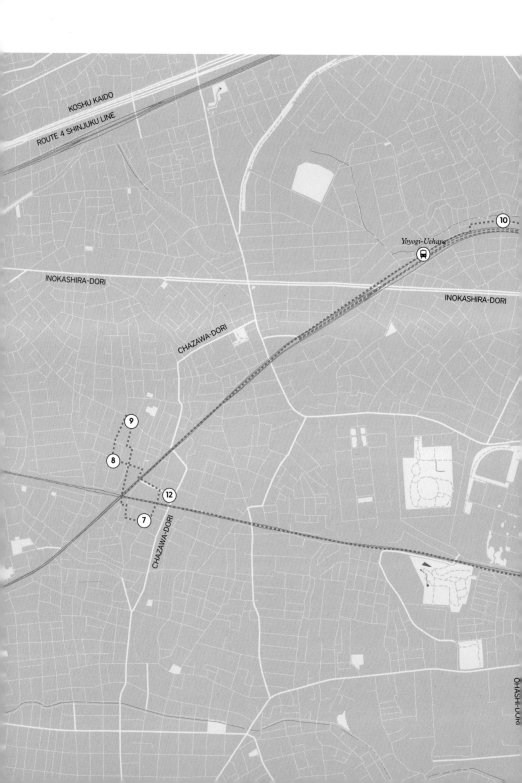

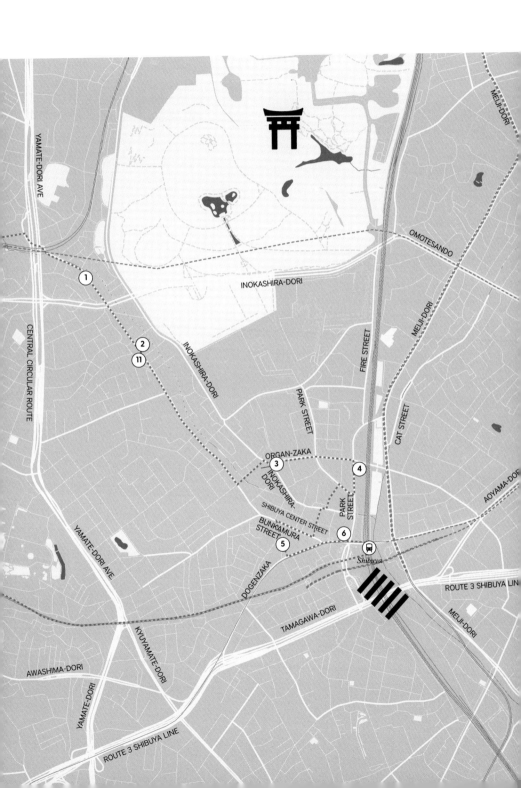

MEIJI-DORI

YAMATE-DORI AVE

CENTRAL CIRCULAR ROUTE

OMOTESANDO

① 1

INOKASHIRA-DORI

② 2
⑪ 11

INOKASHIRA-DORI

FIRE STREET

MEIJI-DORI

PARK STREET

CAT STREET

ORGAN-ZAKA

③ 3

INOKASHIRA-DORI

④ 4

PARK STREET

SHIBUYA CENTER STREET

PARK STREET

YAMATE-DORI AVE

BUNKAMURA STREET

⑥ 6

AOYAMA-DORI

⑤ 5

🚉 Shibuya

DOGENZAKA

ROUTE 3 SHIBUYA LIN

KYUYAMATE-DORI

TAMAGAWA-DORI

MEIJI-DORI

AWASHIMA-DORI

YAMATE-DORI

ROUTE 3 SHIBUYA LINE

VINTAGE FUN ON THE CHUO LINE

FULL-DAY ITINERARY

The Chuo line is one of Tokyo's main rail arteries, a track that runs from Tokyo station to Shinjuku, and then on through the city's western suburbs. It's past Shinjuku that it gets interesting, as the Chuo line links up the likes of Nakano, Koenji, Ogikubo and Kichijoji, some of the city's best locales, particularly if you're into vintage shopping or manga and anime culture. This itinerary provides a range of experiences, from the mind-boggling displays of collectables at Mandarake in Nakano to the vintage stores of Koenji and the bustle of Kichijoji's friendly nightlife.

10AM Begin your day by taking the train to Nakano, which is an easy skip on the Chuo line from Shinjuku. After alighting, take the north exit and wander straight to ① **Nakano Sun Mall**, which tends to open around 10am. This is a classic Tokyo shotengai, a traditional shopping street that has been around since the 1950s, and still seems like a throwback to simpler times.

11AM From the Sun Mall, continue walking north through the quiet streets of Nakano to ② **Araiyakushi Baishoin** (see p.75), a lovely Buddhist temple and garden complex.

11.30AM Walk south back to Nakano Broadway, an admittedly fairly shabby shopping centre that nonetheless contains a whole world of interesting goodies, everything from second-hand kimonos and yukatas to vintage watches and fruit, vegetables and seafood. The top two levels also house the incredible network of shops that are ③ **Mandarake** (see p.187), with various outlets dedicated to every type of collectable imaginable. Note that Mandarake doesn't open until midday. Afterwards, walk back to Nakano station and catch a train one stop to Koenji.

1PM It's time for a little vintage shopping in Tokyo's capital of old-school cool. From Koenji station, take the south exit and walk over to ④ **Whistler** (see p.125), where you'll find all manner of leather shoes, jackets and other paraphernalia from the '50s and '60s. Then walk past probably several hundred more vintage stores (seriously) on your way to ⑤ **Be-In Records** (see p.130), a great vinyl shop on the Look Street shotengai. Afterwards, walk north back to the station to take a train to Ogikubo.

2.30PM Grab a late lunch at ⑥ **Harukiya** (see p.85), a ramen store that has been dishing out some of Tokyo's best noodle soup since 1949. Work off lunch by taking a gentle stroll west, following the train line to Nishi-Ogikubo, where you'll be able to call into ⑦ **Mitsuya Saketen** (see p.203) to delve into the world of sake (plus pick up a bottle or two).

3.30PM From Mitsuya, it's just a short walk to the Nishi-Ogikubo train station, where you'll catch a ride one stop west to Kichijoji and take the south exit. It's a 5-minute walk then to ⑧ **Inokashira Park** (see p.218), a beautiful place to sit down in the sun and relax. Once you have your energy back, take the short stroll to ⑨ **Skit** (see p.133), Kichijoji's epicentre for sneaker heads, before grabbing a quick coffee and admiring the artworks at ⑩ **Cafe Zenon** (see p.158).

5PM Walk west from Cafe Zenon, with the Kichijoji train station on your left, until you see a towering Uniqlo store: this is the entrance to ⑪ **Nakamichi-dori** (see p.169), a street full of designer boutiques, homewares stores and art and craft shops. There's plenty of fun to be had just walking up and down here and calling into any store that looks interesting.

7PM It's time for dinner, which means a very short walk over to Showa-dori, another pedestrianised street, to eat at ⑫ **Satou** (see p.63). This is a well-known butcher that has a restaurant upstairs serving premium Matsusaka wagyu steaks, a must-try in Japan. No booking required here.

8PM Kichijoji's best nightlife is just around the corner, at the ⑬ **Harmonica Yokocho** (see p.87). Try not to fill up too much on steak, because Japanese people tend to snack while they're drinking, and most of the standing-room-only bars along this network of tiny alleys serve food with their beers and spirits. Call in anywhere you like – the bars here are all good. Be careful, however: the last train back to the city leaves Kichijoji just before 1am.

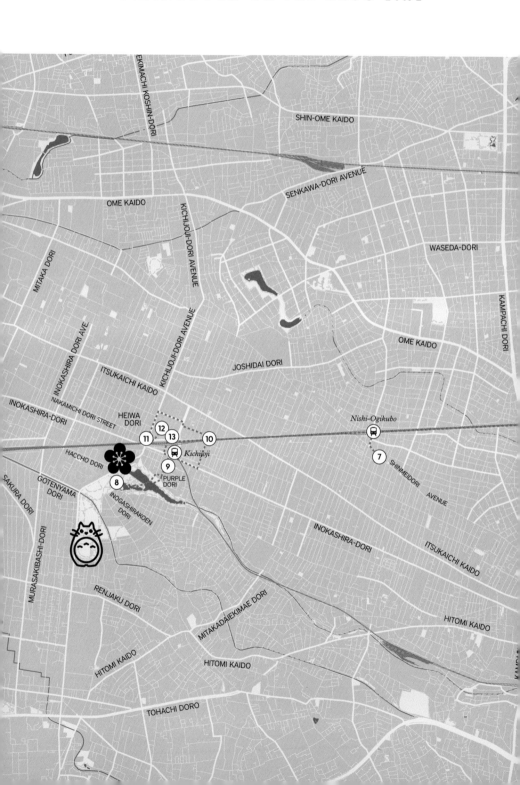

TOKYO'S TRENDY
SOUTH-WEST
FULL-DAY ITINERARY

*You've probably never heard of Gakugei-Daigaku, which is reasonable.
Not only is the name a mouthful, but this quiet neighbourhood in Tokyo's
south-west has largely flown under the radar until recently. Now, however,
thanks to some great shops, excellent donuts and craft beer, 'Gakudai' takes
a rightful place on this south-western itinerary, joining the more established
likes of Meguro and Nakameguro for a day of strolling, nibbling and
sipping in some of Tokyo's most pleasant and easy-going locales.*

10AM Your day begins at Nakameguro train station, an easy ride from
the likes of Shibuya or Ebisu. Exit via the east gate, and take a pleasant
stroll through quiet neighbourhood streets to reach ① **Onibus Coffee
Nakameguro** (see p.110), the home not just of one of Tokyo's finest flat
white–style coffees, but also a lovely spot to sit in the shade and rest up
for the day ahead.

11AM If your visit coincides with cherry blossom season – usually around
April – this is the perfect place to view the sakura (cherry blossom), along
the ② **Meguro River** (see p.215), which is also known as Nakameguro
Canal. From Sidewalk Stand it's easy to reach the river and then follow its
path for as long as you like.

12PM Nakameguro's excellent ③ **J'antiques** vintage store (see p.149)
throws its doors open at the leisurely time of midday, so you'll have to hang
around until then to take the 5-minute stroll over from Onibus Coffee and
begin sorting your way through all of the predominantly American garments
sourced from around the world.

1PM It's definitely time for lunch, so head back to Nakameguro station and
catch the Toyoko line to Gakugei-Daigaku. From there take the east exit and
walk a leisurely 5 minutes to ④ **Bigiya Ramen** (see p.46), home of one
extremely good noodle soup, and perhaps the best ramen egg around.

2PM Dedicate your afternoon to checking out Gakudai's excellent boutique
shops, including ⑤ **Book and Sons** (see p.156), with its great range of
art- and design-focused titles, and ⑥ **Yuyujin** (see p.52), which stocks
excellent artisan-made ceramics from around Japan. Make time to call into
⑦ **Higuma Doughnuts** (see p.151) for a donut and a coffee.

4.30PM What better way to rest weary limbs than with a soak at a genuine Tokyo sento (communal bathhouse)? ⑧ **Tiyo no Yu** (see p.70) is in central Gakugei-Daigaku, an easy stop during any exploration of this neighbourhood, and the perfect place to lay back in warm, mineral-rich waters for an hour or so.

6PM Next, walk a whole one minute to the adjacent street to balance out the health benefits of your sento experience with a few craft beers at ⑨ **Tsukinowaguma** (see p.208). Tokyo doesn't have a huge amount of craft beer – partly because Japan's mass-produced stuff is so good – and this is the ideal spot to sample a few different brews from around the country.

8PM Finally, it's dinner time. This is going to require a ride on a Tokyo bus, so get your map app out and make your way to a bus stop to catch a number 01 or 06 bus to the Otori Jinja Mae stop near Meguro River. Alight and walk about 5 minutes south-east to ⑩ **Sushi Rinda** (see p.99), which provides one of the most enjoyable high-end sushi experiences out there. Make sure you have a booking, bring plenty of cash and know what the etiquette is (see p.227). This will be a highlight of your Tokyo trip.

TOKYO'S TRENDY SOUTH-WEST

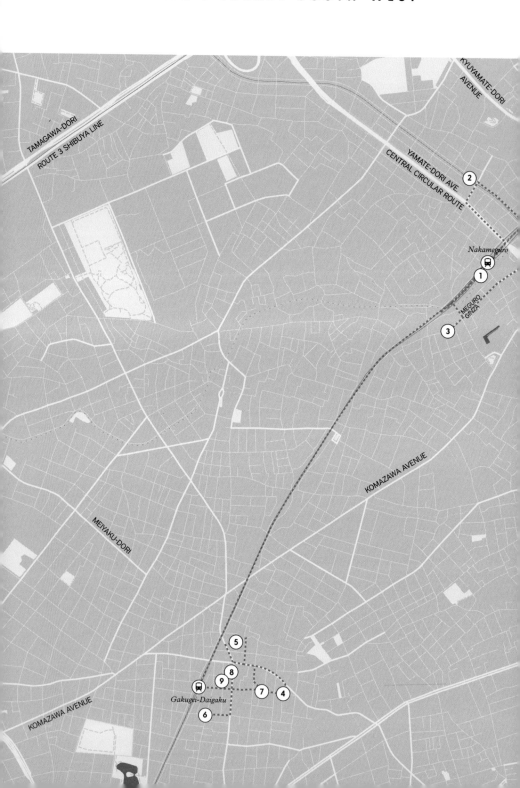

MEIJI-DORI

GAIEN NISHI-DORI

KOMAZAWA-DORI

ROUTE 2 MEGURO LINE

PLATINUM STREET

MEGURO-DORI

YAMATE-DORI AVE.
CENTRAL CIRCULAR ROUTE

ROUTE 2 MEGURO LINE

HANABUSAYAMA STREET

Otori Jinja Mae

YANAGI DORI

MEGURO AVE.

10

YAMATE-DORI AVE.
CENTRAL CIRCULAR ROUTE

SHOKUNIN

There's a long history in Japan of artisanal passion and brilliance, a culture that stretches back centuries to ceramics supplied to royalty, to swords made for samurai, and to food perfected by obsessives nationwide. What sets Tokyo apart is the incredible dedication of its shokunin, its craftsmen and women, their relentless pursuit of perfection, their drive to innovate and yet preserve tradition in their chosen fields.

If you're chasing works of artisanal beauty to bring home as keepsakes, this is the city for you. In most suburbs you will find at least a few artisans who have come close to perfecting their craft, whether they deal in fabrics or pottery, in metalware or food. For the highest concentration, however, stroll around Kuramae, or check out Gakugei-Daigaku.

Regardless of where you are, you will notice a similar dedication among the artisans involved: a knife isn't just a tool in Japan – it's a work of art; a meal isn't mere sustenance – it's performance; a bowl isn't just something to eat from – it's a statement of origin and of ideas. This quest for perfection makes for excellent shopping, and amazing eating. Enjoy.

Eigetsu

詠月

*A centrally located kaiseki restaurant that provides a window
into a complex and beautiful style of cuisine.*

Kaiseki isn't just food – it's art. It's a degustation-style multi-course meal that takes diners on a journey, one that speaks of the season, of the location, of the skill of the chef and of the dedication of those who supply the restaurant with ingredients. This is also a style of Japanese cuisine that can be difficult for foreigners to access for a variety of reasons: the restaurants are often hard to find; they're usually exclusive and almost impossible to book; and the food is difficult to interpret and appreciate without sufficient explanation.

That's what makes Eigetsu, a beautiful kaiseki restaurant in central Akasaka, so good. There's certainly an exclusive feel to a restaurant that only seats 10 people, particularly one with classic wooden counters, sliding paper doors and bamboo screens; however, you can book here through the website Table All, which facilitates reservations in a range of difficult-to-access Tokyo eateries. The entire booking and payment is done online.

Once inside Eigetsu, you will also discover that chef Hidenori Iwasaki speaks English, and will help guide you through his spectacular Kyoto-style kaiseki cuisine, with dishes ranging from raw seafood and rich hot-pots to seared beef. You will need a good amount of time for this and a good amount of money – but it will be worth it.

3-11-7 Akasaka,
Minato-ku

Mon–Sat 6–8.30pm

JP¥
¥ ¥ ¥ ¥

W
tableall.com

Akasaka

Bigiya Ramen

麺処 びぎ屋

Behind an unassuming facade lies one of the best bowls of ramen in Tokyo's south-west.

2-4-9 Takaban, Meguro-ku

3-5722-1669

Gakugei-Daigaku

Wed—Mon 11.30am—2.45pm, 6—9pm

JP¥

¥

Bigiya, in trendy Gakugei-Daigaku, is part of the recent wave of ramen as an art form. It's a relatively modern shop helmed by chef Takatoshi Chouryou, who serves chewy ramen noodles with a deeply complex and delicious chicken- and fish-based shoyu (soy-sauce) broth, as well as various accompaniments that are works of artisanal beauty in their own right.

The restaurant itself is a small, no-frills affair, with ordering via a ticket machine near the door. Press a button for the house specialty, the 'shoyu ramen zenbu iri', and you'll receive a steaming bowl of noodles and broth topped with a slice of chicken that has been marinated for 24 hours and roasted, a slice of pork that has been soaked in a secret sauce and charred, and an egg that is so creamy and umami-rich that it will spoil every egg you ever eat from now on.

If you visit Bigiya in autumn or winter, look out for the chance to add some yuzu – the cherished Japanese citrus – to your broth for extra brightness.

M+

エムピウ

This small shop stocks unique, Italian-influenced leather-goods made by a local artisan.

3-4-5 Kuramae, Taito-ku

Kuramae

Mon–Sat 11am–7pm

JP¥

¥¥

W

m-piu.com

Tokyo's passionate community of artisans often seek to learn their crafts from the best in the business, and if the best isn't in Japan, they will travel. And so, of course, it comes as no surprise to find that leather-goods maker Yuichiro Murakami spent time in Italy learning how best to craft his favourite material.

Though Murakami's training is Italian, his line of wallets, bags, notebooks, slippers and other leather-goods has a distinctly Japanese feel, with functionality to go with the unique and beautiful aged-leather designs created for the M+ label. Murakami has a shopfront in crafty Kuramae, a tranquil space in which to browse the handmade items and decide on your souvenir of choice.

Hokkaido Dosanko Plaza

北海道どさんこプラザ

A Yurakucho mall houses a mouth-watering selection of the finest produce from Hokkaido.

2-10-1 Yurakucho, Chiyoda-ku

Yurakucho

Mon–Sun 10am–8pm

JP¥
¥

W
dosanko-plaza.jp

Ever wanted to travel around Japan without leaving the confines of Tokyo? Easy. Just call into one of the many 'antenna stores', shops that sell produce, arts and crafts and souvenirs from specific prefectures around the country. Along the way you can also pick up travel ideas, chat to locals from specific regions, and eat at restaurants that specialise in regional dishes.

Though these antenna stores are spread throughout Tokyo, there's a large glut located in Kotsu Kaikan, a fairly shabby shopping mall in Yurakucho, a small pocket of southern Ginza. There are shops here for Osaka, Oita, Toyama and more, but by far the most popular is Hokkaido Dosanko Plaza, which specialises in the much-sought-after produce and handicrafts of this island prefecture. Don't miss the melon-flavoured soft-serve ice-cream, which attracts huge crowds, the Royce chocolate-covered potato chips, and the excellent selection of Hokkaido dairy products, as well as the Hokkaido-only Sapporo Classic beer.

Mokuba Showroom
木馬ショールーム

High-end ribbon maker that will be heaven for any lover of DIY.

4-16-8 Kuramae, Taito-ku

Kuramae

Mon–Fri 9am–12pm, 1–5.30pm

JP¥

¥ ¥ ¥

W

mokuba-ribbonline.com

There's a feeling you start to get after wandering around Tokyo for a few days, after exploring the city's boutiques and outlets: Japan has the best of everything. There's so much on sale here that's the pinnacle of whichever niche or obsession you're investigating.

At Mokuba Showroom, a glass-fronted store on the streets of artsy Kuramae, you will discover some of the world's finest ribbon. This is a world-class brand that was founded by Shoichi Watanabe in 1967, and now supplies ribbon to the likes of Louis Vuitton and Dolce & Gabbana. The Mokuba Showroom features a mind-boggling display of the company's beautiful products, all available for purchase, in every size, design, colour and texture you could ever imagine. The ribbons come, of course, at a hefty price, which is going to make wrapping any presents with them a serious commitment.

Shokunin

Kyubey

久兵衛 京王プラザホテル店

*This classic high-end sushi restaurant will wow you
from start to finish.*

Of all of Tokyo's contributions to the world of food, surely sushi is the most famous. This is a style of cuisine now enjoyed around the world, and yet it began in the Japanese capital, and it has been perfected in the Japanese capital.

Kyubey is one of Tokyo's most famous high-end sushi restaurants, something of an empire that spans a main shop in Ginza, and outlets in four luxury hotels. That may make it seem less exclusive than the likes of Sushi Saito or Sukiyabashi Jiro (helmed by he of *Jiro Dreams of Sushi* fame), and yes, it is – but that also means you can get a booking, and you can afford to dine here.

The experience at Kyubey is simply incredible. This outlet at the Keio Plaza in Shinjuku is small and quiet, with guests huddled around a wooden counter as the chefs prepare piece after piece of some of the world's finest seafood, each morsel draped over vinegared rice that you soon realise really is the true star of the show. Kyubey's original owner, Hisaji Imada, is credited with inventing the 'gunkanmaki', or battleship sushi roll, so expect to be served a few of those, probably filled with salmon roe or sea urchin, in your set meal here. Ensure you book ahead.

9
2-2-1 Nishishinjuku,
Shinjuku

Mon–Sun 11.30am–
2.30pm, 5pm–9.30pm

JP¥
¥ ¥ ¥ ¥

W
kyubey.jp/en

☎
3-3344-0315

Nishi-Shinjuku-ku

Shokunin

Yuyujin

釉遊人

Artisanal works from across Japan feature at this cute ceramics store in Gakugei.

3-4-24 Takaban, Meguro-ku

3-3794-1731

Gakugei-Daigaku

Tues–Sun 11am–7pm

JP¥

¥ ¥

W

yuyujin.com

Dine at any reasonably nice restaurant in Japan and you will realise the importance and the beauty of local ceramics. Every plate, every cup, every bowl – even the rest for your chopsticks – has been handmade with love and attention, chosen by the chef so that it's just so. This is one of Japan's oldest art forms, dating back to the Neolithic period, and modern-day artisans, and people who buy their work, are keeping the craft alive.

Yuyujin is one such supporter of local producers, a compact but lovely shop in Gakugei-Daigaku that specialises in handmade, unique ceramic items, as well as others made from glass, lacquer, wood and enamel. Pieces come from across Japan and have been expertly curated, which means you won't have to look too closely to find the perfect plate, bowl, cup, vase or more.

Fuku Yakitori

炭火串焼 ふく

Immerse yourself in the charred, flavoursome world of high-end grilled chicken at this Yoyogi joint.

3-23-4 Nishihara, Shibuya-ku

Yoyogi-Uehara

Thurs–Mon 5.30–11.30pm

JP¥

¥¥

sumibikushiyakifuku.com

For every style of Japanese food, there is a scale. It doesn't matter if you're talking sushi, katsu, tempura or ramen, there are restaurants that turn out cheap, simple versions, there are restaurants that take things more seriously and charge accordingly, and there are those who welcome customers who appreciate their brilliance and perfection. Fuku is the latter.

Fuku is a bustling but friendly yakitori (barbecued chicken – yakitori literally means 'grilled poultry') joint in suburban Yoyogi-Uehara, and here they take their craft very seriously. You can try superbly cooked skewers grilled to perfection over 'binchotan' coals: sample classics such as chicken hearts, chicken 'butts', meatballs of chicken, or chicken wings; or get a little more adventurous with lightly grilled oysters, enoki mushrooms wrapped in bacon, or green peppers filled with melted cheese. Sensational.

Shokunin

mAAch ecute Kanda Manseibashi
マーチエキュート神田万世橋

The name is a mouthful, but the collection of artisans peddling their wares here makes it worth the journey.

1-25-4 Kanda Sudacho, Chiyoda-ku

3-3257-8910

Akihabara

Mon–Sun 11am–9pm

JP¥

¥ ¥

W

ecute.jp/en

Your one-stop shop for boutique, artisanal products is housed underneath a railway line. That may seem odd until you realise that plenty of similar spaces across Tokyo have been utilised for various interesting purposes: restaurants, shops, izakaya (local sake bars) and night-time entertainment areas. So, really, the most baffling thing about mAAch ecute Kanda Manseibashi is the name.

Here you'll find not just a great cafe set on a disused train station platform, with commuters whizzing past on all sides, but also a long row of pop-up stores and artisanal boutiques underneath, selling everything from handmade jewellery and tricked-out audio gear to designer fashion and crockery. There's also Hitachino Brewing Lab, an onsite microbrewery that's perfect for a cleansing ale after an ill-advised shopping spree.

Katsudonya Zuicho

かつどん屋 瑞兆

This tiny family-run katsudon joint takes chicken on rice to another level.

41-26 Udagawacho, Shibuya-ku

Shinsen

Mon–Sat 11.30am–6pm

JP¥

¥

Look for the queue and you're in the right place. Katsudonya Zuicho is a tiny shop down a narrow alleyway in a fairly residential part of trendy Tomigaya. However, among locals it is known: this place does a seriously good katsudon.

This is a dish that should be basic, honest, no-frills (much like Katsudonya's cramped interior). It's just a fried pork cutlet sitting atop scrambled egg and a bowl of rice. The pork is perfectly cooked, tender on the inside and crisp on the out. It sits atop a light, fluffy egg mixture infused with dashi and soy and mirin. Below is a bowl of high-quality rice, with pickles on the side and a bowl of stock-like soup.

This shouldn't be a meal that's elevated to hero status, but after a trip to Katsudonya Zuicho you will understand the obeisance.

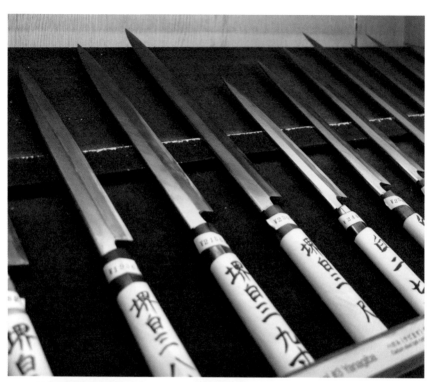

Kama-Asa

釜浅

The heritage of samurai culture is apparent in Japan's beautifully crafted knifeware.

It's not difficult to divine the origins of Japan's knife-making culture. Metal blades have been crafted in this country for centuries: once to arm the samurai, the nation's military nobility, and later to fit out its equally dedicated cooks and chefs. Japanese knives are famous the world over for their quality, their durability and their beauty, and this is the place to stock up if you enjoy spending time in the kitchen.

Set a few blocks away from touristy temple, Senso-ji (see p.69) in Asakusa, Kappabashi Kitchen Street is a strip of shops that sell everything a cook or restaurant owner could ever want: from pots and pans to crockery and chopsticks, from chef's outfits to the plastic models of food you see outside certain restaurants. Around the middle of the street you will find Kama-Asa, a knife-maker founded in 1908, a beautiful shop that sells both Japanese and Western-style knives in a range of sizes and price-points. You can even have your initials carved into your blade of choice. Check out upstairs, as well, for high-end cooking utensils.

Nearby, Kamata and Tsubaya are also excellent knife shops.

2-24-1 Matsugaya, Taito-ku

Mon–Sun 10am–5pm

JP¥

¥ ¥ ¥

W

kama-asa.co.jp

Asakusa

Fukamachi

*Next-level tempura is being dished out at this famed restaurant
in the backstreets of Ginza.*

This is bucket-list dining. The work of culinary fantasy. The stuff dreams are
made of. You may think you know tempura; you may think you have a fair
grasp on just how far one could go with food that is dipped in batter and
fried in oil. But until you visit Fukamachi, a modest-looking but still Michelin-
starred eatery in the backstreets of Ginza, you know nothing.

First, a quick history lesson. Tempura was not technically invented by
the Japanese. The process of battering and frying meat and vegetables was
introduced by Portuguese explorers who were residing in Nagasaki in the 16th
century. So the Japanese didn't come up with this style of cooking, but they
most definitely perfected it. Forget that soggy, gluggy stuff you've had in your
home country: at Fukamachi the very freshest, most seasonally appropriate
fish, seafood and vegetables are dipped in lighter-than-air batter and then
fried in high-quality oil until they're just cooked, crisp on the outside and
steamed perfectly inside.

During a set course of tempura at Fukamachi you will be guided through
the full gamut of what is possible with this style of cuisine. Everything is
amazing, though keep an eye out in particular for the sea urchin roe wrapped
in shiso leaf. Bookings are essential and note that set menus at lunchtime are
significantly cheaper than dinner.

2-5-2 Kyobashi, Chuo-ku

3-5250-8777

Tues–Sun 11.30am–2pm,
5–8.30pm

Tokyo

JP¥
¥ ¥ ¥ ¥

Maito
Design
Works
natural dyeing and
made in Japan

open / 11:30 - 18:30   close / mon

Maito

*A Kuramae atelier that uses a traditional dyeing method
to produce unique fabrics.*

There's a deep respect for nature in Japan that you find cropping up in all sorts of places: in the way people clasp their hands together and say 'itadakimasu' before a meal to say thanks, not just to the cook but to the Earth for providing their sustenance; in the manic way people gather around cherry trees to photograph the blossoms every spring; and even in the way clothes are made.

'Kusaki-zome' is a traditional fabric-dyeing technique in which natural liquids are extracted from flowers, leaves, stems and roots to colour bolts of cloth. The practice is admittedly not as popular as it once was; however, there are still people like Maito Komuro, a clothes maker who has an eponymous store in the suburb of Kuramae, who are continuing the tradition. At Maito you will find a large range of shirts, dresses, bags and scarves dyed using natural kusaki-zome techniques – plant-based fashion at its finest.

4-14-12 Kuramae,
Taito-ku

Tues–Sun
11.30am–6.30pm

JP¥
¥ ¥

W
maitokomuro.com

Kuramae

Satou

吉祥寺さとう

*Some of the world's finest wagyu beef is sold and cooked
at this Kichijoji institution.*

Can a steak be artisanal? Most definitely, when you take into account the
dedication and obsession that goes with breeding and rearing beef cattle
in Japan. Wagyu is something of an artform, and there are three main styles
that are most sought after: Kobe wagyu, perhaps the most famous; Omi
wagyu, from the Shiga prefecture in central Japan; and Matsusaka wagyu,
from the Mie prefecture, also quite near Kobe. From these three areas come
the beef that has that essential marbling the Japanese love, rich ribbons of
fat that run through the meat and cause this stuff to be so highly prized the
world over.

At Satou, a butcher and steakhouse in the suburb of Kichijoji, you can
join the inevitable queue to buy one of the famous minced beef croquettes,
or you can head upstairs to dine on Matsusaka wagyu, cooked on the teppan
plate right in front of you. Matsusaka wagyu, however, comes at a price.
You're looking at up to ¥50,000 or ¥60,000 per kilogram. That may seem
excessive, but bear in mind that only a few thousand of these animals are
slaughtered each year.

There's little fanfare here, despite the quality of the produce. And the
taste? Like no other steak you've tried before. This place is an institution for
a reason.

1-1-8 Kichijoji, Musashino-ku	Butcher: Mon–Sun 10am–7pm; Restaurant: Mon–Fri 11am–3pm, 5–9pm; Sat–Sun 11am–9pm	JP¥ ¥¥¥
4-2222-3130		W shop-satou.com
Kichijoji		

Shokunin

REKISHI

It's easy to see only Tokyo's modern side, the flashing lights, dinging bells and rumbling trains. But the city also pays respect to its history, continues its traditions and honours its past while barrelling full-tilt into the future.

Tokyo's rekishi, its history, takes a little effort to seek out. It's often hidden among towering skyscrapers or cast out into the smaller suburbs. However, if you want to embrace the city once known as Edo – as much a state of mind as a point in history – in the same way its citizens do, it's easy enough to find.

Look closely and you'll discover Buddhist temples and Shinto shrines, peaceful, beautiful places that provide a window into Tokyo's still vibrant spirituality. Stroll around and you will see classic shotengai, the old-style shopping streets made popular in the 19th and 20th centuries. You will discover restaurants that have been open for hundreds of years; bathhouses that continue Japan's famed onsen culture; and workshops that pass on the skills of the past, the likes of swordfighting, taiko drumming and the arrangement of flowers.

To discover Tokyo's past is to find yourself at peace, to take a break from the bustle and to enjoy throwbacks to another, simpler time.

Meiji Jingu

明治神宮

Hidden in the woods near busy Harajuku, this shrine is the perfect symbol of Tokyo's past.

One of the most famous shrines in Tokyo presents something of a paradox: its parkland setting and the nature of the shrine itself should offer a peaceful alternative to the bustling city; however, the popularity of Meiji Jingu among tourists and locals alike means a visit here is rarely a relaxing experience. Still, it's worth battling the crowds, particularly on a warm day, to see this important part of Tokyo's history.

Set close to Harajuku train station, next to the leafy confines of Yoyogi Park (see p.217), Meiji Jingu is a sprawling complex dedicated to the deified spirits of Emperor Meiji, who ruled Japan in the late 19th and early 20th centuries, and who presided over the Meiji Restoration, during which Japan modernised and Westernised and became a global power. To understand the respect with which the emperor is still held, check out the huge torii gates that mark each side of the temple: this is serious stuff and also an excellent photo opportunity.

While visiting the Shinto shrine, visitors can make offerings, buy charms, write down their wishes on small pieces of paper, or keep an eye out for the many traditional wedding ceremonies that take place here. Arrive early to beat the crowds.

📍 1-1 Yoyogikamizonocho, Shibuya-ku

🕐 Mon–Sun 5am–6pm

JP¥ Free

🚃 Harajuku

W meijijingu.or.jp

Senso-ji

浅草寺

*Tokyo's oldest temple is the perfect place to tap into the city's
spiritual side.*

Senso-ji is perhaps Tokyo's most important religious site – and, unfortunately, everyone knows about it. This Buddhist temple complex in historic Asakusa should be peaceful and charming, though you will find it anything but if you visit in the afternoon or early evening. People. Everywhere. For the best of Senso-ji, try to arrive early in the morning, and skip past Nakamise-dori, the historic shopping street that these days is filled with touristy tack, in favour of making your way directly to the main sprawl of buildings.

The Senso-ji complex was completed in 645 CE, making it Tokyo's oldest (though the buildings had to be reconstructed after World War II). On the site, there's a sprawling and beautifully designed main hall, a five-storey pagoda, and a smaller Shinto shrine. After grabbing a few photos of the pagoda and checking out the twin 'Nio' statues – traditional guardians – in the hall, make your way over to a stand by the side of the temple, where you can read your fortune on the 'omikuji' papers (draw a wooden rod from a container to decide which numbered box to pull your fortune from). And then, get out of here.

2-3-1 Asakusa,
Taito-ku

Mon–Sun

JP¥
Free

W
senso-ji.jp

Asakusa

Tiyo no Yu

千代の湯

Soak away your cares at this beautifully revamped sento in Gakugei.

2-20-3 Takaban, Meguro-ku

3-3712-1271

Gakugei-Daigaku

Tues–Sun 3.30pm–1am

JP¥

¥

W

tiyonoyu.com/tiyonoyu.html

Tiyo no Yu is hidden away in the backstreets of Gakugei-Daigaku, a nondescript facade that houses a recently revamped and quite lovely bathhouse. This is a sento, (communal bathhouse), in which you'll be lying back in warm, artificially carbonated waters (said to help with relaxation) with any number of your new and completely naked Japanese friends, surrounded by deep-blue tiling and traditional artwork in an immaculately clean space.

Just remember to shower and soap yourself down thoroughly before entering (BYO soap), don't wear any swimwear into the bath, go into the right section (it's split between a men's side and a women's side) and ensure you don't have any tattoos (they are banned in most sentos due to Yakuza organised crime connections).

HiSUi Tokyo
ヒスイトウキョウ

Learn ancient arts such as 'batto', or sword-fighting, at this Ginza dojo.

4-3-13 Ginza, Chuo-ku

1-2066-6107

Ginza

Mon–Sun 11am–8.30pm

JP¥
Y Y

W
en.hisui-tokyo.com

Every movement has a meaning. The way you stand and rise up on your toes, ready for battle. The way you place your hands on the katana, or traditional samurai sword, and draw it. The way you hold it in front of you, poised and ready. The steps you take forward. The swing and the hiss of the katana in the air.

This is the ancient art of sword-fighting, or at least it's a class at HiSUi. Here, beginners are taken through the very basics of the batto art, beginning with the simple draw of a sword, and ending – if you're skilful enough – with the chopping in half of a bamboo mat. Not bad for 45 minutes' work.

HiSUi offers training in other traditional Japanese arts as well, the likes of kimono dressing, calligraphy and tea ceremony preparation. However, it's the batto class that will stick with you the longest.

Namiki Yabusoba

並木藪蕎麦

A cherished culinary tradition lives on at this 100-year-old soba noodle restaurant.

You could dedicate an entire book to the history and the intricacies involved in the production of soba noodles, one of Japan's most famous dishes. These thin strands of boiled buckwheat were popularised during the Edo period, from the 15th to 18th centuries, and take enormous skill and dedication to produce. Soba noodles also remain one of Tokyo's most popular dishes, a classic stomach-filler than can take the form of a warming soup in winter, or a tray of cold noodles dipped in soy-based sauce during summer.

To get in touch with the Edo roots of soba, call into Namiki Yabusoba, a more-than-100-year-old institution in the heart of Asakusa. This restaurant could so easily be a tourist trap, given its location near Senso-ji (see p.69), and its setting in a historic house, with tatami-mat floors and low wooden tables; however, Namiki is the real deal, turning out hearty, delicious 'yabusoba' – noodles dipped in a thick soy-based reduction, using recipes handed down through generations – day after day. It's eternally popular with both locals and visitors, so expect a queue, though it will move quickly.

And a final local tip for any soba restaurant: when you've finished your noodles, pour some of the 'sobayu', the water the noodles were cooked in, into the dipping sauce and drink it up.

2-11-9 Kaminarimon, Taito-ku

Fri–Wed 11am–7.30pm

Asakusa

3-3841-1340

JP¥

¥

Araiyakushi Baishoin

新井薬師 梅照院

Beat the bustle of Nakano with a stroll around this peaceful temple complex.

Tokyo may seem as if it's all skyscrapers and neon lights, but the city actually has plenty of the temples and shrines more commonly associated with the likes of Kyoto and Nara. Though the most popular of these is probably Senso-ji (see p.69), there are far more pleasant and peaceful spots to enjoy Japan's traditional spiritual culture.

Araiyakushi Baishoin is a Buddhist temple hidden in the backstreets of otaku-friendly Nakano, a tranquil complex that was founded back in the 1500s, and which will take you far from the madding crowds and into the 'real' spirituality of Tokyo.

Locals call past here regularly to pray – the temple is said to be best for those suffering eye ailments or who need help raising children – while the odd tourist will call past just to have a poke around. Araiyakushi Baishoin is especially popular during spring, when the complex's cherry trees erupt into full bloom. This isn't a site with expansive grounds or any 'wow'-inducing monuments, but rather a local-favourite temple in which to spend a little moment of time in peaceful contemplation, before diving right back into Nakano's hectic lifestyle.

If you visit on weekends, keep an eye out for locals selling fruits, vegetables and small household items in the temple grounds.

5-3-5 Arai, Nakano-ku

Mon–Sun 9am–5pm

Araiyakushi-mae

3-3386-1355

JP¥
Free

Dote no Iseya

土手の伊勢屋

A century-old specialist tempura restaurant keeping the spirit of old Tokyo alive.

1-9-2 Nihonzutsumi, Taito-ku

3-3872-4886

Minowa

Thurs–Tues 11am–2.30pm

JP¥

¥

W

dotenoiseya.jp

Some restaurants are as much about the setting as they are the food, and Dote no Iseya is one of them. Set in slightly-sleazy Minowa, it's housed in a traditional wooden building that has somehow survived modernisation. You'll feel like you're in your long-lost Japanese grandmother's loungeroom, thanks to the mismatched furniture, the boxes stacked in unwieldy places, and the ever-friendly waitstaff of advancing age.

This isn't fancy tempura or delicate bites. It's 'ten-don', a whopping bowl of rice topped with equally whopping pieces of battered, deep-fried vegetables and seafood, designed to feed the hungry masses – the workers who have been calling through here since 1873. They know what they're doing here and they do it well. It's a throwback to Edo times – without the frills.

Edo-Tokyo Open-Air Architectural Museum

江戸東京たてもの園

This alfresco museum of houses and buildings shows Tokyo the way it once was.

3-7-1 Sakuracho, Koganei

Musashi-Koganei

Tues–Sun 9.30am–4.30pm

JP¥

¥

W

tatemonoen.jp

Museums display many things, but they rarely show off entire buildings. The Edo-Tokyo Open-Air Architectural Museum, in Tatemono Park in Tokyo's west (an offshoot of the larger Edo-Tokyo Museum), is an outlier there, a refreshing change if you feel like you've been there and done that with museums. Here, whole buildings – historic and important relics of Edo-era Tokyo, as well as prime examples of various classic architectural styles – have been transported and reconstructed.

You'll find everything from an 18th-century farmhouse once inhabited by the noble Yoshino family, to a stunning 1940s mansion designed by architect Kunio Maekawa, and the Art Deco Tokiwadai Photo Studio building, originally constructed in the 1930s.

The Edo-Tokyo Museum is another excellent facility featuring numerous exhibits from Tokyo's Edo period, and a little easier to access, near tourist-friendly Asakusa.

Café de l'Ambre

カフェ ド ランブル

Japan's kissaten coffee culture is taken to another level at this historic Ginza institution.

8-10-15 Ginza, Chuo-ku

3-3571-1551

Higashi-Ginza

Wed–Mon 12pm–9.30pm

JP¥

¥ ¥

Café de l'Ambre is a classic kissaten (old-style coffee shop) that opened in 1948 and has been serving coffee – and only coffee – ever since. Though most kissaten in Tokyo tend to offer more charm than quality when it comes to the beverages, Café de l'Ambre is different. Here, coffee is obsessed over and has been perfected over the years, with beans carefully sourced from around the world, painstakingly roasted and meticulously prepared for each customer. You can select the quality of beans you prefer, with everything from 'green label', the cheapest, up to 'gold'.

Though plenty will come to Café de l'Ambre for the history, for the old-Tokyo vibes and the old-Tokyo clientele (including, if you know what you're looking for, the odd celebrity or two), they will leave endlessly impressed by the drinks.

Taiko-Lab

浅草

Tap into the primal power of Japanese taiko drumming at this Asakusa school.

3-4-9 Asakusa, Taito-ku

Asakusa

Mon–Fri 9.30am–10pm,
Sat 9.30am–8pm,
Sun 9.30am–6pm

JP¥

¥ ¥

W

taiko-center.co.jp

If you've ever attended a Japanese festival or ceremony, you're probably familiar with taiko (traditional drums). Taiko date back to at least the 6th century, and have been used through history as musical instruments, theatrical accompaniments and calls to war; the drums are often works of art themselves.

Though it's unlikely you'll take home an entire taiko as a souvenir, you can tap into taiko culture by taking a one-hour introductory lesson at Taiko-Lab. There's something beautifully primal about drumming, about beating out a tattoo on one of the world's oldest instruments. It's also a huge amount of fun to grab a pair of bachi (drumsticks) and go to town on a range of instruments.

Note that at time of printing, the tourist-focused Asakusa location of Taiko-Lab was actually closed, with future plans unclear once international tourism resumes. Check the lab's website before visiting, or call past its Aoyama location (3-1-30 Jingumae, Shibuya-ku).

Happo-En

八芳園

A teahouse set in an Edo-era garden provides the perfect opportunity to sample matcha.

1-1-1 Shirokanedai, Minato-ku

Shirokanedai

Mon–Fri 10am–8.30pm;
Sat–Sun 9am–8.30pm

JP¥

¥¥

W

happo-en.com

Within a stone's throw of the bustling Tokyo streets is Happo-En, a tranquil Edo-era garden and teahouse in Meguro, a world away from the modern metropolis.

It's a joy just to stroll around this facility that is believed to have once been the home of 17th-century samurai Tadataka Okubo. There are koi ponds, cherry trees, pines, gold-leafed maples, bonsai trees, and stone carvings that make perfect Insta-fodder.

The real treat, however, is the traditional teahouse sheltered among the pines, where you can take part in a traditional Japanese tea ceremony. Cross your legs on the tatami-mat floor and prepare for an elaborate ritual that involves the measuring of matcha powder, the careful whisking, and the pairing with intricately designed wagashi (sweets). And afterwards, relax.

Ohara School of Ikebana

Embrace the gentle art of Japanese flower-arranging at this friendly Omotesando school.

5-7-17 Minamiaoyama, Minato-ku

Omote-Sando

Mon–Sun 10am–4pm

JP¥

¥¥

W

ohararyu.or.jp

Look around you in any traditional house in Japan, any upmarket restaurant or classic hotel: somewhere there will be an alcove decorated with a few carefully chosen and seasonally significant flowers. As with any Japanese artform, ikebana (flower-arranging), is taken very seriously, and it's done with a style and beauty that's unique to Japan.

And of course, you will want to learn how to do it yourself. Ohara School of Ikebana is a venerable institution founded by Unshin Ohara in 1912, and one that passes on the tradition of Japanese flower-arranging to dedicated students and casual passers-by alike. Here you can take anything from a five-year masters' course to a five-hour introductory lesson, conducted in English (bookings required).

All tools and materials are provided; all you'll need to bring is enthusiasm.

Tonki

とんき

*A venerable institution that has been dishing up deep-fried
pork – and little else – for more than 80 years.*

The Japanese didn't really invent katsu, the breaded, deep-fried hunks of
pork so loved across the nation, the same as they didn't really invent tempura
and they didn't really invent gyoza. However, as with most of the foreign
foodstuffs the country's cooks and chefs have turned their hands to, they
certainly perfected it. Inspired by European breaded cutlets – cutlet became
kutsu, which in turn became katsu, and an obsession was born – tonkatsu has
become a phenomenon all of its own, a thick slice of either fatty or lean pork
fillet that's dredged in panko crumbs and deep-fried until golden and crisp,
served with a sweet, tangy sauce, mustard, shredded cabbage and rice.

One of the pioneers of the katsu craze was Tonki, a much-loved
Meguro institution that first slid its wooden doors open in 1939. Here the
panko crumbs are ground into a fine powder before coating the pork, which
gives the crust a much smoother texture than other modern versions of katsu,
but it's still absolutely delicious, with high-quality pork that's remarkably
tender. If you judge on food only, there are better katsu restaurants in
Tokyo – try Butagumi in Nishi-Azabu, or Narikura in Takadanobaba – but
Tonki is one of the originals, a bare-bones restaurant that consists solely of a
huge U-shaped wooden bar surrounding an open kitchen, with an old-school
atmosphere – and clientele – that's as enticing as its cuisine.

1-1-2 Shimomeguro,
Meguro-ku

Wed–Mon 4–10.45pm

Meguro

3-3491-9928

JP¥

¥ ¥

Nezu Museum
根津美術館

Set amid a traditional garden in upmarket Omotesando, this is your spot for viewing ancient artefacts.

6-5-1 Minamiaoyama, Minato-ku

Omote-Sando

Tues–Sun 10am–5pm

JP¥

¥

W

nezu-muse.or.jp

Here's a museum that's as interesting for the building itself as for its contents. It was designed by award-winning architect Kengo Kuma (also responsible for Tokyo's new Olympic stadium), and it's set on the grounds of what was, up until 1940, the home of Tobu Railway President Nezu Kaichiro, an avid art collector. The gardens are immaculately sculpted, with several ponds and streams, and the museum building itself makes the most of its tranquil setting with bamboo-lined walkways and a glass frontage.

Inside, you'll find the private art collection of Kaichiro-san, with more than 7000 objects of pre-modern Japanese and East Asian art on display. These include paintings, calligraphy, ceramics and textiles, all of which give context to the modern arts and crafts you will see around you in Tokyo today.

Harukiya

春木屋 荻窪本店

This Ogikubo ramen joint takes a cherished staple dish back to its roots.

1-4-6 Kamiogi, Suginami-ku

Ogikubo

Mon–Sun 11am–9pm

JP¥

¥

W

haruki-ya.co.jp

Ramen wasn't always a thing of otaku-level nerdery and scientific analysis, despite what you may find on Tokyo's streets today. There was a time when ramen was just noodle soup, hearty and delicious. One of the throwbacks to that era is Harukiya, a ramen honten (shop), in Ogikubo. It has served Tokyo-style soy sauce–based ramen since 1949, and it's still owned by Kouichi Imamura, son of founder Itsuo Imamura.

The recipe here is decades-old: the soup base is made using dried sardines, adding extra umami, and served with curly, hand-rolled noodles, pickled bamboo, nori and pork.

This is one of Tokyo's cheapest bowls of ramen, yet it's incredibly high-quality, and a pleasant blast from the city's past.

Harmonica Yokocho
ハーモニカ横丁

*A maze of narrow alleys in Kichijoji hosts traditional drinking dens
with real character.*

Tokyo is a big, anonymous city that does friendly small-bar culture better than almost anywhere. For proof, simply wander down one of its many yokochos, networks of inner-city alleyways that are lined cheek-by-jowl with tiny drinking holes and smoky izakaya (local sake bars), with punters shuffling shoulder-to-shoulder between them. Some of the best-known of these can be found in popular nightlife areas such as Shibuya and Ebisu; however, for a feel of 'real' Tokyo, head to either Koenji Street, a strip of bars underneath the railway tracks in Koenji, or better yet, the character-soaked Harmonica Yokocho in Kichijoji.

This is a yokocho with history, a series of tiny alleys that functioned as a local flea market in the 1940s, and in the last few decades has reinvented itself as a nightlife hotspot full of cheap-and-cheerful bars and izakaya, many of which can fit only about 10 standing patrons at a time. Though you'll have a great experience calling into any of the establishments here, keep an eye out for Katakuchi, which does great sashimi, and Minmin, famous for its gyoza dumplings.

📍 1-1 Kichijoji Honcho, Musashino-ku

🕐 Various

JP¥ ¥

🚌 Kichijoji

Sumo

This ancient sport allows a window into Japanese history and culture – as well as making for an entertaining afternoon.

As with so many aspects of Japanese culture, you could take sumo wrestling at face value – two fat guys pushing each other around for fun – or you could look a little deeper into the true meaning. For option B, Tokyo is your city, any time of year. Sumo is both a sport and an artform that dates back more than 1000 years, and today it is still imbued with so many historical rituals and traditions, from the top-knot hairstyles of the wrestlers to the tossing of salt and the stomping of feet before a bout.

The only way to really understand sumo is to attend a tournament, though unfortunately these only take place three times a year in Tokyo (Jan, May and Sept), all held at the Ryogoku Sumo Hall near Asakusa. If your visit coincides with a tournament, you will be able to secure tickets through the website listed below.

If you're in town at any other time, it's still possible to tap into sumo culture by calling past the Arashio-beya Sumo Stable, the main training centre for professional wrestlers, which allows members of the public to watch their sessions (via a window from the street) from 6.30am until 10am most mornings.

Ryogoku Sumo Hall: 1-3-28 Yokoami, Sumida-ku; Arashio-beya: 2-47-2 Nihonbashi Hamacho, Chuo-ku

Ryogoku Sumo Hall: Jan, May and Sept; Arashio-beya: Mon–Sun 6.30–10am

JP¥

2500–20,000 JP¥

W

sumo.pia.jp/en; arashio.net

Ryogoku; Hamacho

Imperial Palace

The Japanese emperor's residence makes the perfect getaway
from the bustle of nearby Ginza.

Tokyo is not a city that can boast too many important historical buildings. If you want castles you go to Himeji or Matsumoto. If you want temples and shrines you go to Kyoto or Nara. There is, however, one building of historical significance worth seeing and that is the Imperial Palace, home of Japan's Imperial Family, and a lovely place to wander, even if the public can't access the inner grounds.

The Imperial Palace was built on the site of the old Edo Castle in 1888; it was destroyed in World War II but rebuilt in the same style soon after. Most of the buildings here have to be viewed from across the moat, given the lack of access for mere mortals such as ourselves; however, guided tours that take in a small section of the inner grounds are held twice a day from Tuesday to Saturday, with advanced bookings recommended. Alternatively, the gardens in the outer grounds – sprawling and classically designed, with plenty of shade on hot days – make a great getaway from bustling Tokyo life.

1-1 Chiyoda, Chiyoda-ku

Tokyo

Gardens Mon–Sun;
Tours Tues–Sat 9am
& 1pm

JP¥

¥

sankan.kunaicho.go.jp

Kabe no Ana
イタリアン & パスタ 壁の穴 渋谷本店

The pioneers of the Japanese 'wafu pasta' genre are still dishing out some fine spaghetti.

2-25-17 Dogenzaka, Shibuya-ku

Shibuya

Mon–Fri 11.30am–10pm, Sat–Sun 11am–10pm

JP¥

¥¥

W

kabenoana.com

Pasta? In Japan? Yes, and yes. The Japanese are masters of the noodle, and pasta is no different. You want to eat pasta in Tokyo. You want to see how a cuisine held firm by tradition in its country of origin is treated with wild creativity here. Japanese ingredients adapted to Italian techniques: what's not to love?

Kabe no Ana, a small shop on a busy Shibuya alley, is credited as being the birthplace of Japan's obsession with pasta, and cooks here began experimenting with spaghetti back in 1963. It sparked an entirely new cuisine – wafu pasta – and Kabe still does it best. Call in for spaghetti served with sea urchin, salmon roe and shredded nori. It shouldn't work. It surely won't work. And yet this is one of the best pasta dishes you will try.

Tsukiji Outer Market

築地場外市場

Street-food stands and retailers battle on at southern Tokyo's former tourist hotspot.

5-2-1 Tsukiji, Chuo-ku

Tsukiji

Mon–Sun 9am–2pm

JP¥

¥

W

tsukiji.or.jp

The tuna auctions are dead; long live the tuna auctions. Sadly, the famous daily sale of some of the world's finest and most expensive seafood has moved from Tsukiji, along with the entire market. The rattling, shabby Inner Market of Tsukiji was shifted to new facilities in Toyosu in 2018. Yes, the early-morning tuna auctions still take place in Toyosu; however, viewing for tourists is behind thick windows which cut a lot of the atmosphere.

To get in touch with the spirit of historic Tsukiji, you can still visit the Outer Market of small retail stores, street-food stands and sushi restaurants. These seafood purveyors once boasted the freshest fish in town; these days, however, they have their produce sent over from Toyosu, the same as everyone else. That makes Tsukiji an interesting place to wander around, though certainly not a unique place to eat.

Mitsukoshi depachika
銀座三越

This traditional food hall is packed with some of the best gourmet goodies from around Japan.

Department stores in Tokyo are not the department stores you know from home. Yes, they sell all of the usual clothes, homewares, perfumes and accessories spread across multiple floors. But it's what's on top and at the bottom that's most interesting.

On the upper two levels of almost every large department store in Tokyo you will find a series of high-quality restaurants, which serve a range of foods and mostly work on a walk-up, no-reservations policy. These places are perfect for families or newcomers to Tokyo who are a little uncomfortable with the challenge of finding a place to eat at street level.

In the basement, you'll discover a culinary paradise: the depachika, a market hall filled with the absolute finest gastronomic delights, from pre-packed lunches and gourmet ingredients to pastries, cakes and desserts. The Mitsukoshi department store in Ginza hosts one of the city's finest depachikas, a sprawling food hall where you'll be able to pick up any number of traditional delights, from high-end seasonal produce like melons and berries (which can go for hundreds of dollars in Japan), to gourmet specialties from around the country. Don't arrive too hungry: you'll blow your travel budget in minutes.

♀	⊗	JP¥
4-6-16 Ginza, Chuo-ku	Mon–Sun 10am–8pm	¥ ¥
🚃		W
Ginza		mitsukoshi.mistore.jp

NYUU-EBU

Forward. Forever forward. That's Tokyo, a city that celebrates
its past and yet is always careening full-tilt into the future;
a megalopolis that is in a constant state of flux, that morphs
and evolves before your very eyes. Fads appear and disappear
in the blink of an eye. Neighbourhoods change. Ideas change.
The only constant is the headlong rush to evolve.

Tokyo is changing, and it's up to you to keep up. That
change might sound like it's dominated by neon and glass,
but in reality the fads of Tokyo are far more organic, and
likely to relate to the city's driving obsession: food. There's
a new wave of cuisine to be enjoyed in Tokyo right now,
from artisanal coffee made by passionate local baristas, to
Japanese spins on much-loved foreign foods, and the dedicated
evolution of dining styles that have existed in the city
for centuries.

If you're ready to embrace change, to jump on this crazy
bandwagon and see where it will take you, you need only
two things: a credit card and an empty stomach.

Sushi Rinda

鮨 りんだ

This charming, relaxed sushi bar takes the intimidation factor
out of high-end dining.

It's easy to feel intimidated by the high-end sushi experience in Tokyo. There are all these rules to follow, mostly unwritten (though see p.227 for a few). You have to turn up bang on time. You don't wear perfume. You don't rest your watch or your phone on the wooden countertop. You eat each piece of sushi within a few seconds of its being presented to you. You respect the chef, respect the craft. It's an amazing experience, but also kind of stuffy.

That is, until you eat at Sushi Rinda. This is high-end sushi with a sense of humour. The itamae (chef) at Rinda is Yuta Kono, who spent part of his early life living outside of Japan, and who speaks excellent English – that's a huge bonus for foreign diners, who so often miss out on the interaction with the itamae, which forms such an integral part of the sushi experience. Throughout the service Kono-san and his team crack jokes, they drink sake, they chat to customers, and without your even noticing, they prepare an absolute feast of high-end seafood, more than 20 courses that take diners on a culinary journey through everything that's possible at a modern-day sushi restaurant.

The food here is traditional and superb, focusing on the finest, freshest seafood. The decor is classically minimalist, with a long wooden bar overlooking the open kitchen, the chefs slicing fish and moulding rice before your eyes. The atmosphere is relaxed and foreigner-friendly, with a gentle hubbub of chatter throughout. In other words, Rinda is perfection.

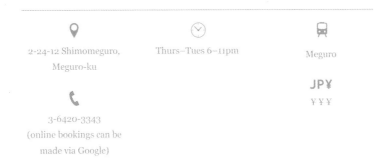

2-24-12 Shimomeguro,
Meguro-ku

Thurs–Tues 6–11pm

Meguro

3-6420-3343
(online bookings can be
made via Google)

JP¥
¥ ¥ ¥

Yuji

ゆうじらーめんとうきょう

Yuji Haraguchi's tuna-bone soup is at the forefront of the
'kodawari' artisan ramen movement.

Saying ramen is just noodle soup is like saying Tokyo is just a city: technically correct, but missing a universe of nuance. Ramen is a genuine obsession in Tokyo. Though the most famous style outside of Japan is probably tonkotsu, the thick, hearty broth made using pork bones, in Tokyo there are now infinite variations – from chicken, dried fish, and now, the boiled bones of the city's beloved tuna.

Yuji Haraguchi is a former salesman turned self-taught ramen master, who opened his first restaurant in the USA before an outlet of his eponymous honten (shop) in Tokyo's east in 2018. Here he serves toothsome noodles with his mellow but complex tuna-bone broth, topped with confit tuna and a slice of citrus. Different, and delicious.

◉	◔	**JP¥**
3-3-25 Kiyosumi, Koto-ku	Mon–Sat 11.30am–2.30pm	¥
	& 5.30pm–9.30pm;	
🚆	Sun 11.30am–7.30pm	**W**
Kiyosumi-Shirakawa		yujiramen.com

Isetan

Fashionistas meet foodies at this upscale department store,
where the true highlight lies underground.

Isetan is all about the new and exciting, befitting the department store's location in ultra-modern Shinjuku. Here you'll find two interconnected seven-storey buildings bulging with designer clothes, cutting-edge homewares and all the accessories you could ever dream of, as well as a rooftop garden and some high-quality restaurants on the top floor.

For the best of Isetan, however, you have to go below street level, to the depachika (food hall) on the first basement level. This is a gastronomic wonderland that embraces the new wave of Japanese gourmet obsession, including not just food from around Japan, but from around the world. You'll find the finest Scottish whiskies next to their Japanese equivalents; beautifully crafted French chocolates and pastries next to local wagashi sweets; difficult-to-source Western ingredients near the best Japanese goods. Foodies could spend a lot of time and a lot of money in this place: it's the ideal spot to stock up for a gourmet picnic in Shinjuku Gyoen National Garden (see p.216) nearby, or to treat yourself to a relaxing night in if you've rented an apartment with a kitchen.

3-14-1 Shinjuku,
Shinjuku-ku

Mon–Sun 10am–8pm

JP¥
¥ ¥

W
isetan.mistore.jp

Shinjuku-sanchome

Afuri

One of the original artisan ramen shops continues to attract the crowds.

1-1-7 Ebisu, Shibuya-ku

Ebisu

Mon–Sun 11am–5am

JP¥

¥

W

afuri.com

Afuri is no secret: it's one of Tokyo's most popular ramen restaurants, with 12 outlets in the greater city area, and it's in the USA and Singapore. However, this is Japan, where standards don't drop when popularity arrives. Afuri churns out reliably good new-wave ramen at all of its stores.

It's famous for its signature yuzu shio ramen, a salt-based broth with zesty yuzu juice, served with char-grilled slices of pork belly and a perfectly cooked egg. If this is your first time at Afuri, that's the dish to order. There are a few tasty variations, and it's one of the few restaurants to offer a vegan ramen option – solid gold in this city of dedicated omnivores.

Hiroki

広島焼き HIROKI 下北沢店

Hiroshima-style pancakes are the order of the day at this Shimokitazawa eatery.

2-14-14 Kitazawa, Setagaya-ku

Shimokitazawa

Mon–Sun 12pm–10pm

JP¥

¥

W

teppan-hiroki.com/
shimokitazawa.html

Tokyo has its own version of delicious okonomiyaki, the Japanese savoury pancake: it's called monjayaki, a thinner, crispier version of chunky okonomiyaki. However, for the newer and more popular version, head to trendy Shimokitazawa, where Hiroki dishes out Hiroshima-style pancakes to the hungry masses.

These guys take their okonomiyaki seriously: the ingredients are all sourced from the Hiroshima area, and the preparation follows that city's unique style, with a layer of batter for the base, topped with shredded cabbage, noodles, pork and egg, which are fried together and then topped with sweet sauce, green onions and your protein of choice: maybe oysters, squid, or more pork. It's delicious, and cooked on hotplates in front of the diners, adding to the relaxed, fun atmosphere.

Maisen

とんかつまい泉青山本店レストラン

*This katsu powerhouse
hasn't let popularity go
to its head.*

4-8-5 Jingumae, Shibuya-ku

Omote-Sando

Mon–Sun 11am–10pm

JP¥

¥¥

W

mai-sen.com/restaurant

This is what modern katsu (breaded pork cutlets) looks like. Maisen has moved from humble beginnings in 1965 to the porky empire that it is today, with 11 restaurant outlets and 62 stands inside department stores selling its famous product.

The good news is that Maisen is famous for a reason, and quality hasn't taken a hit with expansion. Head to Maisen's main store in fancy Aoyama, set in an old public bathhouse, and you'll be able to enjoy a bit of history with your thoroughly modern katsu, with the choice of a few other menu items that are breaded and fried and served with shredded cabbage and rice. Get here early to avoid the bulk of the queues.

Bear Pond Espresso

ベアーポンドエスプレッソ

The welcome isn't exactly warm but the coffee is excellent at this Shimokita institution.

2-36-12 Kitazawa, Setagaya-ku

Shimokitazawa

Wed—Mon 10.30am–6pm

JP¥

¥

W

bearpondespressoroasters.com

They don't like you at Bear Pond Espresso. They don't like me, either. The service at Bear Pond is notoriously surly: owner Katsuyuki Tanaka clearly cares deeply about coffee, and perhaps not so deeply about customer service. There are signs at Bear Pond saying photography is banned; others warn you against sitting down with a laptop. Just drink your damn coffee.

So why is Bear Pond appearing in these pages? Because the coffee is great. Superb. This is third-wave coffee with something extra, espresso with a deeply complex flavour, a pleasant chocolatey nuttiness that you just don't get from any other cup. Don't come here for the service. Don't come here for the atmosphere. Do come here for truly great coffee.

Pizza Studio Tamaki

*A Tokyo-trained pizziaolo is turning out some
of the best pies around.*

Italian food is big in Japan, as it is everywhere in the world. In Tokyo now there
are Italian-style cafes popping up everywhere, pasta restaurants serving Italian
classics and Japanese-inspired dishes, and a spate of pizza joints that take
their pies very seriously. There's often little room for reinvention here: Tokyo
residents like their pizzas in the legit Neapolitan style, with spongy crusts and
soupy centres, and toppings that have made their way directly from Italy.

One of the best purveyors is Pizza Studio Tamaki, a small restaurant
that feels like a slice of Italy – high wooden tables and chairs and a bar
overlooking the wood-fired oven – in a quiet area of Azabu, helmed by pizziaolo
Tsubasa Tamaki. The pizzas here are cooked in a searing hot oven for only
a minute or so, and arrive topped with ingredients mostly sourced from Italy,
though with a few house-made additions available.

If it seems odd to be eating pizza in Tokyo, know this: when the
Japanese set their minds to making something, they make it incredibly well,
and Pizza Studio Tamaki is no different.

1-24-6 Higashiazabu,
Minato-ku

Mon–Fri 5pm–11pm,
Sat–Sun 12pm–4pm &
5pm–10pm

JP¥

¥ ¥

W

pst-tk2-ad.com

Akabanebashi

Onibus Coffee Nakameguro

オニバスコーヒー 中目黒

Local coffee roaster and importer provides the perfect hideaway to enjoy a good cup.

2-14-1 Kamimeguro, Meguro-ku

Nakameguro

Mon–Sun 9am–6pm

JP¥

¥

W

onibuscoffee.com

Onibus is your little slice of peace in busy Nakameguro, the perfect place to grab an excellent coffee, relax and then get back to the serious business of shopping and eating. This boutique coffee roaster and cafe is right near Nakameguro station, set in a renovated old house, with plenty of terrace seating on wooden benches, and a playground next door – ideal for those attempting to tame their kids while enjoying a caffeine hit.

The menu is simple: espresso, Americano, latte or hand-drip filter coffee. This narrow range of options means everything is done extremely well. The beans are imported from Rwanda and Guatemala, roasted on site, and prepared via a La Marzocco espresso machine or a Hario V60 drip filter.

Coffee Supreme

Kiwis bring their excellent brand of new-wave coffee to the backstreets of Tomigaya.

42-3 Kamiyamacho, Shibuya-ku

Yoyogi-Hachiman

Mon–Sun 8am-7pm

JP¥

Ұ Ұ

W

coffeesupreme.com

There's something about the Tomigaya neighbourhood, near Shibuya, that makes you think there will be good coffee here. Maybe it's all the moustachioed hipsters riding fixed-gear bikes; maybe it's the boutiques selling impossibly cool homewares; maybe it's the cafes sporting Italian-style espresso machines. Probably the latter.

Coffee Supreme is a friendly little joint with a minimalist fit-out. This third-wave coffee outlet has an antipodean connection: Coffee Supreme is a New Zealand company that roasts beans at its home base in Wellington. The cafe also sells a small range of brunch-friendly snacks, which can be surprisingly difficult to find in Tokyo.

Grab a flat white–style coffee, grab a seat, and watch the uber-cool world of Tomigaya pass you by.

T's TanTan

T's たんたん グランスタ東京
（京葉ストリートエリア）

Vegan ramen? It's a thing, deep underground in Tokyo station,
and it's delicious.

In a city where anything goes, where progress is constant and reinvention is assumed, it can be a little hard to stand out from the crowd. That's especially true for ramen restaurants: some estimate that there's more than 10,000 of these establishments in Tokyo alone. So how do you make your mark?

At T's TanTan, it's by stripping away everything you think you know about ramen and starting again. Namely: taking away the meat. This is a vegan ramen store, a shop serving entirely plant-based versions of soups that are usually made with pork bones or dried fish and topped with more pork, and usually an egg. Not so at T's, which is somewhat hidden in plain sight in the bowels of Tokyo train station. Here, surprisingly rich, complex soups are created using vegetables, miso and sesame oil, with toppings such as soy 'mince', shredded green onions, pumpkin seeds and even walnuts.

Note that T's TanTan is inside the gates at Tokyo station (the nearest entrance being JR Yaesu South), which means you will need to be travelling by JR train to get to the restaurant.

♀	⊘	**JP¥**
1-9-1 Marunouchi, Chiyoda-ku	Mon–Sun 7am–10.30pm	¥
		W
🚇		ts-restaurant.jp/tantan
Tokyo		

OUT

This Shibuya institution is a hyper-niche pasta joint serving up delicious food to a soundtrack of Led Zeppelin.

Only in Tokyo could you have a restaurant so narrow in its offerings, so unashamedly niche. At OUT they serve just one truffle-flavoured pasta dish, just one type of red wine, and the soundtrack features just one band, Led Zeppelin. That's it.

The Australian co-owner, David Mackintosh, likens his concept eatery to a haiku, a poem with seemingly strict rules but infinite possibilities.

The restaurant's name is inspired by the Led Zep record 'In Through the Out Door', and it's likely you'll hear a few tracks from it as you huddle around the 12-seat bar and order your truffle pasta and wine from the ramen-style vending machine. The pasta, of course, is superb. The wine is excellent. And the music? It's your stairway to heaven.

2-7-14 Shibuya, Shibuya-ku	Tues–Sun 6–10.30pm	JP¥ ¥¥
Shibuya		W out.restaurant

Nyuu-ebu

Path

Breakfast lovers, rejoice: here's a cafe that opens early and caters to all your morning needs.

Breakfast is an eternal problem for visitors to Tokyo, which is something of a head-scratcher given everyone in this city enjoys eating so much. And yet, no one seems to be out and nothing seems to be open at the beginning of the day. Plenty of cafes don't even begin service until 11am or midday. This is not a place where locals linger over morning cuisine.

Fortunately, there are a few answers for hungry travellers, one of which is Path, a third-wave coffee joint in hipster Tomigaya. Here the coffee is great, as you would expect, the service is friendly, and the breakfast offerings are almost peerless: the croissants and pain au chocolat could have come straight from Paris, and the heartier offerings such as eggs Benedict and granola bowls will gladden the heart of any weary, hungry traveller. Even the cafe's Euro-style fit-out, with exposed lightbulbs hanging over low wooden tables, will be recognisable to brunch-lovers.

Come lunchtime Path really kicks into gear, with excellent Western-style offerings cooked with Japanese flair, and dinner is similarly good; however, for most visitors this place is all about breakfast.

1-44-2 Tomigaya, Shibuya-ku	Tues–Sun 8am–2pm, 6–11pm	Yoyogi-Hachiman
3-6407-0011		JP¥ ¥ ¥

Vintage

BINTEJI

For a city so focused on the future, there's a surprising embrace of the past in Tokyo. Not just the distant past, but the past that's near enough to remember but worth trying to forget: the '70s, '80s and '90s, which in Tokyo have now been curated to fit the modern day, their most embarrassing misjudgements forgotten and their glories properly celebrated. The hipper residents of Tokyo love an item with a story, something that has made its way across the world, something that can be repackaged with a modern sensibility and treasured once again.

The most obvious sign of that is the market for vintage clothing, and it really is huge in the likes of Koenji, Shimokitazawa and Kichijoji, where you will find store after store. There is, however, more to the vintage obsession than mere threads. Vinyl records are loved and celebrated here. Vintage photography equipment is in demand – collectors will love Lemon Inc (see p.121). Old-school arcade and video games are very much de rigueur. And you can even pick up vintage eyewear at Solakzade (see p.135), from as far back as the 1800s. If you appreciate the style and the tastes of bygone eras, Tokyo is your town.

Lemon Inc
レモン社 銀座教会店

This consignment store is heaven for those interested in vintage camera gear and old watches.

Photography nerds, pack your credit cards and head directly to Lemon, a vintage camera and accessories store in an office block high above fancy Ginza. If you've ever wondered where you can pick up that mint-condition '70s Leica 50mm lens, it's Lemon. If you're hunting a genuine Hasselblad 1000F camera body from the early '50s, there's every chance you will find one here. This store is an absolute treasure trove for photography enthusiasts, where everything is sold on consignment, everything is in excellent condition, and everything costs a lot of money.

It's not just camera gear either, but all sorts of collectables, most of which tend to appeal to people of a certain vintage themselves: fountain pens, model cars and trains, binoculars, eyeglass frames. The store also stocks an impressive range of high-end vintage watches from brands such as Rolex, Omega, Seiko and Citizen.

Lemon is a little tricky to find (use a map app, look for the picture of the lemon out front, and head to the 8th floor), but well worth the effort for those who love their gadgets.

📍 4-2-1 Ginza, Chuo-ku

🕐 Mon–Sun 11am–8pm

JP¥ ¥¥¥

🚇 Ginza

W lemonsha.com

Disk Union
ディスクユニオン

*A sprawling series of Shinjuku venues plays host to a truly
mind-bogglingly array of vinyl records.*

Vinyl never died in Tokyo. These old-style records might be going through
a hipster-led resurgence in the rest of the world but in the Japanese capital
they just never went away: in a city of obsessives, where music is just as
highly valued as anything else, vinyl provides the best quality for listening to
your favourite jams. And the best place to source those records, hands-down,
is Disk Union, a sprawling beast of a store that spans 11 venues in Shinjuku
alone, each space and each level dedicated to a different style of music.

    Begin your search at the main Disk Union store near Shinjuku
Sanchome station, where eight floors are packed with vinyl, with everything
from rock to Latin to prog to punk. Then, choose your poison: there are shops
dedicated to jazz, to classical, to soul, to hip-hop, to heavy metal and more.
All of the records have been meticulously assessed, categorised and labelled,
and each bears a price tag to reflect its quality and rarity. Be careful: that
album you're holding in your hands might cost $5, or it could be $500.

📍	🕐	JP¥
3-31-4 Shinjuku, Shinjuku-ku	Mon–Sun 11am–9pm	¥¥
🚉		W
Shinjuku Sanchome		diskunion.net

Whistler

Vintage leather is the speciality at this wide-ranging
Koenji boutique.

Where is the epicentre of the Tokyo vintage clothing scene? You could argue that it's in Shimokitazawa, which has an embarrassment of interesting, eclectic stores. Except, you would be wrong. Because it's in Koenji. This neighbourhood west of Shinjuku is a vintage lover's dream, with store after store to stumble upon, with somewhere in the region of at least 60 or 70 shops that specialise in everything from shoes to sunglasses, denim to leathergoods, band T-shirts to books, Americana to old-school Japanese. If this sounds like your jam, then set aside at least a day to wander the streets of Koenji and discover.

Of course, I can't profile every single store here, so just know this: Koenji's vintage scene is roughly split into two areas, south-east and south-west, which relate to their position relative to the train station, with Konan-dori as the central axis. The south-west is bigger and better known, though there are some great finds in the south-east, including Whistler, an American vintage store that specialises in workwear and army clothing from the '40s to the '60s. You will spot Whistler from a mile off thanks to the large racks of used leather shoes outside; step into the store and you'll discover tightly packed rack after tightly packed rack of leather jackets, dress shirts, flannel shirts, jeans, T-shirts, ties and other accessories. Whistler's clothing is predominantly for men, though women will also find a rack or two to sift through.

4-30-8 Koenjiminami,
Suginami-ku

Koenji

Mon–Sun 12pm–9pm

JP¥

¥ ¥

W

whistler-and-chart.
amebaownd.com

Binteji

Bar Track

Ebisu 'listening bar' divides opinions, but it's the perfect drinking den for vinyl aficionados.

3-24-9 Higashi, Shibuya-ku

Ebisu

Mon–Sun 7pm–3am

JP¥

¥ ¥

W

martha-records.com/track

Shhh. If you're deemed to be making too much noise in Bar Track, you might be asked to leave. That's because this is a 'listening bar', a place vinyl obsessives visit to enjoy the best music, chosen by owner Waturu Fukuyama from his library of more than 6000 records and played on the finest vintage equipment, tube amps and Tannoy speakers that sound spectacular (even in a bar).

Some people love Bar Track (and its sister establishment, Bar Martha) and some people hate it. It's not always the friendliest joint, but if you drink whisky – Track has an excellent selection – and you have a passion for music, from the Stones to the Clash to the Chili Peppers, you will love Track. Just, be quiet.

Flamingo
フラミンゴ 下北沢店

Classic used-clothing store offers hours of browsing through rack after rack of treasures.

2-25-12 Kitazawa, Setagaya-ku

Shimokitazawa

Mon–Fri 12pm–9pm,
Sat–Sun 11am–9pm

JP¥

¥

W
flamingo-online.jp

The hipster-friendly suburb of Shimokitazawa has no shortage of vintage clothing stores. Check out New York Joe or Toyo Hyakkaten for huge and varied ranges of vintage gear; or go to Ocean BLVD for a chaotic collection of vintage and handmade clothing and accessories.

Alternatively, head to Flamingo, one of the original Shimokita vintage stores, and where the prices are friendly and the garments well chosen. Flamingo stocks mostly American clothes, shoes and accessories that date back to the '60s. The store is a little chaotic and it can be hard to get your bearings at first, but give it time. Sift through the flannel shirts, military jackets, woollen sweaters and old T-shirts and you'll be in heaven.

Super Potato
スーパーポテト 秋葉原店

Colossal vintage gaming store in Akihabara that is almost single-handedly keeping Mario Bros. alive.

1-11-2 Sotokanda, Chiyoda-ku

Akihabara

Mon–Sun 11am–8pm

JP¥

¥¥

W

superpotato.com

If you believe that computer gaming peaked at Super Mario Bros. or you miss your old Power Glove, then this place is for you. In fact, if you enjoyed any sort of electronic entertainment in the late '80s and early '90s, Super Potato will be your new favourite venue.

This shop harks back to when Game Boys were the height of gadgetry sophistication, and everyone knew who Ryu and Chun-Li were. Super Potato has everything from Sega Mega Drives and Super Nintendos to Atari 7800s, plus all of the games and accessories (including Power Gloves). Even if you don't plan to buy, it's worth browsing and playing a few games of Legend of Zelda or Super Mario Bros. in-store.

Flash Disc Ranch

フラッシュ・ディスク・ランチ

Eclectic Shimokita record store offers a great range of affordable vinyl.

2-12-16 Kitazawa, Setagaya-ku

Shimokitazawa

Mon–Tues & Thurs–Fri
12pm–10pm, Sat 3–9pm,
Sun 2.30–9pm

JP¥

¥

Owner Masao Tsubaki has been running friendly Flash Disc for almost 40 years, and the store has the feel of someone's garage, with street-art and band posters on the walls, and cardboard boxes filled with an array of records and other paraphernalia. If it seems a little intimidating, fear not: Masao-san speaks good English and is always happy to steer customers in the right musical direction.

He also stocks an excellent and affordable range of music, spanning rock, soul, jazz, garage, R&B and 'oldies'. Keep an eye out for the bargain bins too, where you can usually pick up a disc for ¥100 – a rarity in Tokyo these days.

Be-In Records

ビー・インレコーズ

This small boutique Koenji record store specialises in all things collectable from the world's biggest bands.

3-57-8 Koenjiminami,
Suginami-ku

Koenji

Mon–Sun 12.30pm–8pm

JP¥

¥¥

W

bein.co.jp

Vinyl-loving visitors to Japan will quickly realise that local collectors have three main obsessions: the Beatles, the Rolling Stones and Led Zeppelin. This legendary triumvirate can account for huge sections of any store, with everything from original pressings to rarities and bootlegs up for grabs at often hefty prices. True aficionados of those three bands, however, will often end up at Be-In Records, absolutely rammed with classic albums.

There are original pressings of classic recordings, rare overseas pressings, and the entire solo catalogues of each individual band member. You'll also find classics from the likes of Elvis, Jimi Hendrix, Pink Floyd and more. About the only difficulty is moving around the store, so full is it with boxes of records.

Toro Vintage Clothing

This painfully cool Harajuku vintage store has done all the hard work for you.

1-2-10 Jingumae, Shibuya-ku

Meiji-jingumae

Mon–Sun 12pm–8pm

JP¥
¥ ¥ ¥

If you love nothing more than sifting through rack after rack of hodgepodge vintage clothes, searching for one treasure in all the trash ... then Toro is not for you. All of the pieces in this uber-cool shop have already been carefully selected by those with a fine eye for vintage fashion. You just have to find something that fits.

The garments here have been painstakingly sourced from the USA and Europe, and go back as far as the 1940s – though most are from the '50s and '60s. You'll find pieces for men and women, from jackets and jumpers to jeans and shoes. You'll have to be prepared, of course, for the cost of looking this cool: there are few bargains at Toro.

Skit
SKIT 東京・吉祥寺店

Sneaker heads, prepare to discover your new favourite place in the entire world.

In wonderful Tokyo, where every niche obsession is respected and catered to, there are plenty of vintage shoe stores. These outlets tend to be in the vintage heartlands, the likes of Shimokitazawa, Koenji and Kichijoji, and they each have their various specialties: vintage skate shoes, old work boots, classic fine leather shoes, and, of course, sneakers. For the latter, sneaker heads should make their way directly to Skit, a sprawling and well stocked store in the backstreets of Kichijoji.

Here you'll find wall after wall of lovingly shrink-wrapped vintage, rare and collectable kicks, from the likes of Nike, adidas, Puma, Reebok, Vans, Converse and Onitsuka Tiger. If you're after a pair of hard-to-find Air Jordans, this is your store. If you're hoping to rock original Reebok Pumps, you will probably find them here. Most shoes are sourced by the pair only, given they're one-off vintage items, so if you find something you like that's in your size, best to snap it up quickly. Check out the locked section at the back of the store for the truly bank-busting high-end rarities.

📍 1-18-1 Kichijojiminami, Musashino-shi

🕗 Mon–Sun 11am–9pm

JP¥ ¥¥

🚃 Kichijoji

W k-skit.com

Solakzade

ソラックザーデ

Vintage eyewear store in Harajuku takes sunglasses
and spectacle frames to the next level.

Take a look around on the streets of Harajuku and you will see plenty of people rocking some pretty out-there eyewear, leading a vintage trend that has since swept the world. Some of those frames are sure to have been sourced from Solakzade, a vintage eyewear specialist run by brothers Tatsuya and Rio Okamoto. The pair have impeccable taste in glasses, and are obsessives in their own right: Tatsuya specialises in sourcing and identifying vintage frames from as far back as hundreds of years ago, while Rio restores them and gets them ready for sale. Both work a side hustle styling eyewear and jewellery for Hollywood and Japanese film projects.

Call past Solakzade to check out more than 10,000 pairs of 'dead stock' vintage eyewear, frames that date as far back as the 1800s, housed in a stylish space with chandeliers hanging above artfully lit display cases that are vintage works of art themselves. Tatsuya's particular obsession is Ray-Ban sunglasses from the 1940s to '90s, so you will find plenty of those for sale, alongside the likes of Christian Dior, Jean-Paul Gaultier and more. Prepare, of course, for price tags that match the exclusive nature of the products.

4-29-4 Jingumae,
Shibuya-ku

Thurs–Tues 2–7pm

JP¥
¥ ¥ ¥

W
solakzade.com

Meiji-jingumae

Binteji

AMERIKANA

It shouldn't be this way, when you think about it. The Japanese shouldn't be so into American culture. These two countries have fought a war. Their cultures are both so strong and yet so diametrically opposed. Americans, generally, don't deal in subtlety. Japanese culture is all about the appreciation of the small, the natural and the ethereal.

And, yet, spend a little time in Tokyo and you begin to realise that American culture is everywhere. It has been absorbed, in many ways, into the local way of doing things, American practices and cultural rites that have morphed into obsessions that are distinctly Japanese. The locals here love baseball: it's one of the most popular sports in the country, though supported and followed in very Japanese ways. American music is popular. American clothes are popular. Even American food – burgers, donuts, bagels – have found their way into the Japanese consciousness.

From the crowds packing into the almost infinite number of American-style convenience stores, to the kids hanging out at Starbucks, to the people queuing up for pancakes: American culture is here, and it's worth celebrating.

Konbini

You'll find everything you could ever need – and plenty you don't – at a Tokyo convenience store.

You may scoff at the idea of calling into a Japanese konbini (convenience store), but you shouldn't: these places are tourist attractions in their own right, cultural staples that will tell you so much about the place you're visiting, and the needs and wants of so many disparate people.

The convenience store concept is surely America's greatest gift to the culture of Japan. It's an idea that has been seized upon and improved, moulded and extended into a vast and almost unknowable network of cheap-and-cheerful shopfronts that stock absolutely everything you could ever need. Plus, the beer is really cheap.

Probably the strangest thing you'll discover in a Japanese konbini is the high quality of the food. No reheated, four-day-old meat pies here. Everything is fresh and delicious, from the onigiri (rice balls) to the salads, pastas, sandwiches, sushi and the gyoza. There are also great on-the-go snacks, as well as every beverage you could ever imagine, including those affordable local beers.

Look out for the likes of 7-Eleven, Lawson and Family Mart: konbinis that will often have public toilets, plus powerpoints for charging devices, and cash machines/ATMs that accept foreign cards. In other words, every traveller's new best friend.

Various (everywhere)

JP¥

¥

W

sej.co.jp; lawson.jp; family.co.jp

Amerikana

New York Bar

There is no shortage of Lost in Translation *moments at this famous hotel bar with one of Tokyo's best views.*

3-7-1-2 Nishishinjuku, Shinjuku-ku

Shinjuku

Sun–Wed 5pm–12am,
Thurs–Sat 5pm–1am

JP¥

¥ ¥ ¥

W

hyatt.com

The reason this bar on the top floor of the Park Hyatt is so famous is because of its starring role in the Sofia Coppola film *Lost in Translation* – compulsory viewing for anyone hoping to get their head around Tokyo. Even without Bill Murray and Scarlett Johansson though, this is Tokyo's quintessential American-style bar. The tinkling piano transports you directly to Manhattan. The incredible sky-high view of Tokyo's lights could almost be New York. The cocktails could be straight from a prohibition-era speakeasy. And the crowd certainly has its share of visitors and expats.

The bar readily embraces the film connection and even has an in-house cocktail called the L.I.T. Sip it with a view to die for.

Shelter

下北沢 SHELTER

Get your toes tapping or your head banging at this legendary Shimokitazawa underground rock venue.

2-6-10 Kitazawa, Setagaya-ku

Shimokitazawa

Mon–Sun 7pm–late

JP¥

¥

W

loft-prj.co.jp/shelter

Tokyo has a huge and passionate live music scene, much of it housed in tiny basement venues called 'live houses'. Shelter is one of the city's classics, a club that has been hosting American-influenced indie and hard rock bands for more than 25 years. Most of the acts are local up-and-comers, though you will recognise the genres, from punk and metal to post-grunge and alternative.

Shelter is set in a small room under an apartment block that was once designed as a bomb shelter, and is appropriately sound-proofed and squeezy. It's smoky and loud, and worth bringing earplugs, even for live-music veterans. Shelter hosts gigs every night of the week, with tickets at the door.

Amerikana

Meiji Jingu Baseball Stadium
明治神宮野球場

*Japan's most popular sport is an American game that has been
moulded to suit local sensibilities.*

Yes, sumo wrestling is officially Japan's national sport. And traditional martial
arts such as karate, judo and kendo still have a special place in the nation's
heart. However, the sport that really stirs modern passions? The one that
truly captures the country's attention? For that you have to look to baseball,
the American sport that reigns supreme in the competition for local hearts
and minds. The locals love a ballgame, and it's well worth getting along
to see what all the fuss is about.

A baseball game in Japan is, as you would expect, a uniquely
Japanese experience. Gone are the hotdogs and the seventh-inning stretch
of the Major Leagues, replaced by groups of supporters who only cheer
when their team is batting; by stadium restaurants that serve karaage and
yakisoba; by traditions that are unique to each team. One of the best of the
latter is practised by the fans of Tokyo's Yakult Swallows, who play at the
historic and charming Meiji Jingu stadium near Harajuku. Every time their
team scores a run, the fans stand up, twirl colourful umbrellas in the air and
sing an upbeat J-pop song.

Be sure to book game tickets in advance. If you arrive in the city
outside baseball season (March to April), it's still possible to soak up the
sport's culture by hitting a few home runs at the Shinjuku Batting Center.

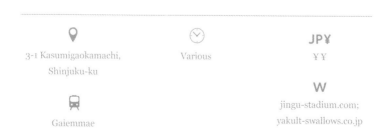

3-1 Kasumigaokamachi,
Shinjuku-ku

Various

JP¥
¥ ¥

W
jingu-stadium.com;
yakult-swallows.co.jp

Gaiemmae

Amerikana

Eight Burger's

Call past this friendly Shimokita joint to sample classic American burgers with a Japanese twist.

2-24-9 Kitazawa, Setagaya-ku

3-5738-8069

Shimokitazawa

Mon–Sun 11.30am–11pm

JP¥

¥

What could be more American than a burger? There are a growing number of artisanal joints taking this fast-food staple to the next level. One of those is Eight Burger's, an industrial-styled space on Shimokitazawa's busy streets.

Though it will drive punctuation nerds crazy (seriously, what is that apostrophe doing in the name?), Eight dishes up some excellent burgers – American classics that have a Japanese twist, everything from standard cheeseburgers to chilli cheese and smoky bacon and mushroom, each topped with kewpie-style mayonnaise and a sweet sauce that tastes a lot like the one traditionally served with katsu. Eight also serves local craft beer, and plays good music. What more do you need?

Haight & Ashbury

Flower power reigns supreme at this vintage stalwart.

2-37-2 Kitazawa, Setagaya-ku

Shimokitazawa

Mon–Fri 1–9pm,
Sat–Sun 12pm–9pm

JP¥

¥ ¥

W

haightandashbury.com

Tokyo's American clothing obsession should be obvious to anyone wandering the streets of Shimokitazawa and Koenji, where store after store is filled with vintage Americana, from old-school jeans and jackets to college T-shirts and military gear.

It's no surprise to find that Haight & Ashbury concentrates its efforts on West Coast American fashion from the '50s and '60s, taking its name from the time that part of San Francisco was the epicentre of the hippie movement. It's not all flower-power in here though, with a section of the store dedicated to vintage that stretches back to the 19th century, as well as a solid collection of jumpers, tees, dresses and shoes from the '80s and '90s.

Amerikana

Sidewalk Coffee Roasters
Coffee & Bagel

Great coffee, plus a legit bagel with a schmear – what more could you want?

3-9-19 Kitazawa, Setagaya-ku

Shimokitazawa

Mon–Sun 7am–7pm

JP¥

¥

W

sidewalk.jp

The Japanese have an impressive custom of taking a foreign food and either reproducing it faithfully, or even improving upon it. At Sidewalk Coffee Roasters (a small local chain with four shops in Tokyo), it's the latter. This Shimokitazawa venue specialises in bagels, which are of New York quality, though with a puffy shape that all but cancels out the annoying hole in the middle. Those bagels come in flavours such as poppy seed, cheese, chocolate, and 'everything', and are all ready to be schmeared with housemade cream cheese and topped with lox.

Sidewalk is set into the side of the smart new Mustard Hotel, an airy, modern location with a big wooden deck outside, about a seven-minute walk from Shimo-Kitazawa train station. The coffee here is roasted onsite, and served third-wave espresso style, or drip.

Starbucks Shibuya

スターバックス コーヒー SHIBUYA TSUTAYA店

There's reason to visit the US's much-maligned coffee chain in Tokyo: the view.

21-6 Udagawacho, Shibuya-ku

Shibuya

Mon–Sun 6.30am–2am

JP¥

¥

W

starbucks.co.jp

America's most famous caffeinated export is also its most divisive – you either love Starbucks or you hate it. The Seattle-based chain was once something of a haven for foreign tourists in Japan, as the forerunner of the second wave, the coffee that came after the old-school kissaten (coffee shop) but before the artisanal espresso.

So, yes, you may love or hate Starbucks. Regardless, the Shibuya store has one huge hook: it commands one of the most important views in all of Tokyo, staring straight over the Shibuya Scramble, the famously busy pedestrian crosswalk. Grab a coffee, take a window seat on the second floor and gawp at the sheer number of people moving through Shibuya at any moment in time.

Tower Records
東急ハンズ渋谷店

It's back to the future at Shibuya's sprawling paean to the humble compact disc.

1-22-14 Jinnan, Shibuya-ku

Shibuya

Mon–Sun 10am–10pm

JP¥

¥

W

tower.jp

It's a measure of Japan's love for music – in its old-school, tangible form, the likes of vinyl records, cassette tapes and CDs – that Tower Records ultimately failed in the USA, its country of origin, and yet continues to thrive in Japan. Tower Records's flagship store boasts a colossal nine floors of music and associated paraphernalia.

This store is like a step back into the '90s, when CDs still ruled. There's a small section for new and used vinyl here, and an even smaller display of used cassette tapes; mostly, however, Tower Records is about the CD, with specialty sections on J-pop, J-indies and K-pop. There's also a cafe and a bookstore.

J'antiques

ジャンティーク

If old-school Americana is your thing, you could spend hours here just wandering and reminiscing.

2-25-13 Kamimeguro,
Meguro-ku

3-5704-8188

Nakameguro

Mon–Sun 12pm–10pm

JP¥
¥ ¥

W
jantiques05.buyshop.jp

If it's antique, and it's American, and it's cool, then J'antiques has it. This hipper-than-thou vintage store on a Nakameguro shopping street is filled to bursting with an amazing array of North American bits and bobs from the 20th century: everything from original denim to dresses and scarves, cravats and ties, bolts of cloth and bandannas, knitwear and skate clothing, old keys and old pins, coats and vintage coat hangers, watches and buttons, chairs and tables … even a decent collection of lava lamps.

J'antiques is run by Hitoshi Uchida, who has a fine eye for beautiful vintage things. His store is large and tightly packed, but everything has been carefully selected and arranged.

Higuma Doughnuts

*Donuts in a lumberjack's cabin? The setting might be odd
by the food is to die for.*

There's almost something funny about the earnestness of this faithful
reproduction of a lumberjack's cabin in suburban Gaku-Dai. The banquette
seats are upholstered in the sort of black-and-red flannel you would expect
to find on a wood-chopper's back, and the interior of the store is lined with
the type of lumber he would have been cutting. It would probably be hilarious,
if the donuts weren't so good. And the donuts here are very, very good.

Tokyo loves a donut. You'll find purveyors of fluffy, circular deliciousness
throughout the trendy west of the city. What sets Higuma apart though is the
use of wheat, milk, butter and sugar from Hokkaido – the island prefecture
in Japan's north where, you soon discover, all the good produce comes
from – to create perfectly springy, airy donuts. They come topped with
cinnamon, chocolate or honey mascarpone, or filled with raspberry or
blueberry jam. The coffee is American-style drip, and goes perfectly with
a sugary treat.

2-8-21 Takaban,
Meguro-ku

Thurs–Tues 10am–9pm

JP¥
¥

W
higuma.co

Gakugei-Daigaku

Amerikana

SEKKEI

Tokyo is all about the clever use of space. Every home here is designed thoughtfully and made to look beautiful, though always efficient. Every large building is laid out to utilise the available area.

This idea of space, however, is not just physical, but one that is used with exquisite precision by Japan's artists and designers: the 'air', or blank space, utilised in traditional woodblock prints and in modern graphic design; in the sparse patterns printed on ceramics; and in the deceptive simplicity of its architecture (walk around Ginza, see p.161, to appreciate a few modern highlights). It takes a while to realise this mastery of space, the way it draws focus to a single, beautiful point. It's seductive and highly skillful, and innately Japanese.

In Tokyo there are some fantastic galleries – like Yoseido Gallery (p.157) – that specialise in everything from traditional masterpieces to works by up-and-coming locals. There's a plethora of museums showing off works by Japan's finest artists. If design to you means clothing, Tokyo is one of the world's fashion capitals, with a host of local boutiques and international mega-stores. And it's a treasure-trove of high-quality art and stationery supplies. Dig in, look around, enjoy. And appreciate the use of space.

teamLab Planets

チームラボプラネッツ

*This visual wonderland blurs the boundaries
between art and nature.*

There's nothing else in the world quite like Planets, an entire museum designed by the hyper-creative teamLab group. It's an immersive, interactive display that fuses art and nature in a way you have never seen before. Picture the four massive exhibition spaces and two gardens here as planets of their own, where the old rules of museums and galleries are torn up, where flowers move and walls sparkle and the world changes with a flick of a switch.

You could lose days in teamLab Planets just staring, photographing and wandering. These are deeply engaging artworks that patrons view barefoot, to encourage a sense of connection with each 'planet'. There's also a vegan ramen restaurant called Vegan Ramen UZU Tokyo on site – meals can either be enjoyed while immersed in a digital exhibition, or outside in one of the garden spaces.

Bring your camera and prepare to go crazy.

♀	◷	**JP¥**
6-1-16 Toyosu, Koto-ku	Daily 10am-6pm	¥
🚃		**W**
Shin-Toyosu		planets.teamlab.art/tokyo

Book and Sons

Delve deep into the world of graphic design and typography in this beautiful space.

2-13-3 Takaban, Meguro-ku

Gakugei-Daigaku

Thurs–Tues 12pm–7pm

JP¥

¥

W

bookandsons.com

There's beauty in the written word, no doubt – though to some people the letters themselves contain the true attraction. If graphic design and typesetting are your idea of art and creativity, then this is the perfect bookstore for you.

Some tomes here are second-hand and others new, but all have a beauty to them that will immediately draw the eye of anyone who has had to design a page or a poster.

The store features a gallery space at the back, where exhibitions of international and local design are often held, and are free to view. There's also a coffee stand, and rotating displays of other artisanal goods. Come here to browse, to buy, or simply to take inspiration.

Yoseido Gallery
養清堂画廊

Take home a unique souvenir at this Ginza gallery, which stocks modern woodblock art prints.

5-5-15 Ginza, Chuo-ku

Ginza

⌄

Mon–Sat 11am–7pm

JP¥

¥ ¥ ¥

W

yoseido.com

Perhaps Japan's most famous style of artwork is the woodblock print, a technique perfected during the Edo period. Japan's woodblock art often captures idyllic rural scenes and people in elaborate dress, compositions that were mastered centuries ago by the famed likes of Hokusai and Hiroshige.

There is still much of this beautiful style of artwork being produced in Japan, and one of the best places to view it – and buy it – is Yoseido Gallery in Ginza. It stocks a large range of high-quality, modern Japanese art, with a focus on woodblock printing. Some pieces follow the traditional style, while others are more avant-garde and daring. The service here is knowledgeable and helpful, and you're sure to walk out with a unique souvenir.

Cafe Zenon

カフェゼノン＆ゼノンサカバ 吉祥寺店

This calming, peaceful space hosts exhibitions of local artists – and does a great coffee.

2-11-3 Kichijoji Minamicho, Musashino-ku

Kichijoji

Mon–Sun 11am–11pm

JP¥

¥

W

zenon-sakaba.jp

Take one look inside Cafe Zenon and you already know the owners care about art and design. Exposed lightbulbs dangle from the ceiling. Original artworks hang from the walls. Books line various shelves. Creeping vines and other plants bring nature to the indoors. The Zenon baristas roast their beans in-house and specialise in 'latte art', drawing creative and kawaii (cute) little pictures in your frothy cup.

Set just a 5-minute walk from Kichijoji station, Cafe Zenon is a haven from the bustle of the streets, a place to enjoy a seasonal curry or pasta dish as well as coffee. There's a revolving cast of local artists' works on show, with a leaning towards manga, though plenty of modern styles are featured.

Mori Art Museum
森アーツセンターギャラリー

Come for the view and stay for the artwork at this sky-high exhibition space.

6-10-1 Roppongi, Minato-ku

Roppongi

Wed–Mon 10am–9.30pm,
Tues 10am–4.30pm

JP¥
¥¥

W
mori.art.museum

Here's an art gallery with dual attractions: visual splendour both on the walls and outside the windows. Mori Art Museum is set on the 53rd floor of the Roppongi Hills Mori Tower, and commands stunning views across Tokyo. It's easy to become distracted by those views, and forget to look at the exhibitions behind you – but that would be a mistake.

Mori Art museum exhibits a revolving series of displays of contemporary works across nine gallery spaces, and has featured the likes of Ai Weiwei and Tokujin Yoshioka. Exhibitions feature a wide range of media, from photography and sculpture to digital art and fashion. The entry price might seem a little steep, but it also entitles entry to the rooftop observation deck.

Ginza Architecture
ギンザシックス

Bold designs and modern materials mark out the impressive architectural works of Tokyo's premier district.

Fans of modern architecture need not head to a museum or even gaze at a book. To witness some of the most forward-thinking and daring designs of the past couple of decades, simply spend time wandering the streets of Ginza with your eyes trained skywards. This is some of the world's most expensive real estate, and it shows.

Begin on Sony-dori at the flagship Hermès store (5-4-1 Ginza, Chuo-ku), the work of Italian master Renzo Piano, who used 13,000 square glass blocks to make the building look like a jewel. From there continue to Ginza Maronie-dori to see the undulating steel facade of the V88 Building (2-5-11 Ginza, Chuo-ku), which reflects the sunlight in ever-changing patterns. Next, turn the corner to see the flagship Louis Vuitton store (3-6-1 Ginza, Chuo-ku), with its Jun Aoki-designed facade modelled on the company's iconic pattern, before continuing on to check out Ginza Six (6-10-1 Ginza, Chuo-ku), quite possibly the world's most impressive shopping mall.

These buildings are some of the finest examples of Ginza's modern architecture boom, drawing the eye as effectively as any local artwork, and all were erected in the last 25 years. For a change of pace, meanwhile, the Okuno Building (1-9-8 Ginza, Chuo-ku), on Ginza Mihara-dori, was erected in 1932, one of Ginza's few surviving pre-war constructions, and now houses a fascinating array of tiny art galleries and boutiques.

📍	🕐	JP¥
Start: Hermès 5-4-1 Ginza, Chuo-ku; End: Okuno Bldg 1-9-8 Ginza, Chuo-ku	Various	Free

🚋
Ginza

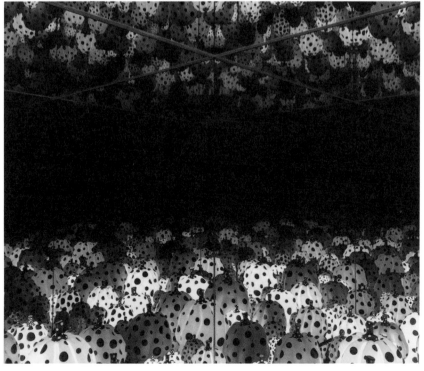

Yayoi Kusama Museum

草間彌生美術館

*Japan's 'brightest' artistic talent has a gallery all of her own
in Tokyo's northern suburbs.*

You already know Yayoi Kusama, even if you don't realise it. If you've ever seen an image of a giant, brightly painted pumpkin, then you're familiar with this idiosyncratic artist's oeuvre. Kusama is something of a legend of the Japanese modern-art scene, a nonagenarian who is still widely respected and admired, someone whose riotously coloured work is instantly recognisable. She's best known for her pumpkins – her black-and-yellow pumpkin on Naoshima Island is iconic – but also paints bright canvases and other media.

The Yayoi Kusama Museum, in Tokyo's northern Bentencho neighbourhood, has been set up to showcase the artist's lifetime of work, from very early pieces to her latest creations. The building itself is impressive, a sleek and slim edifice designed by local firm Kume Sekkei, and commands a good view of the Tokyo skyline from its rooftop; however, it's the artworks that people come here for, including those signature pumpkins.

Bookings have to be made online, and should be done well in advance.

📍	🕐	JP¥
107 Bentencho, Shinjuku-ku	Thurs–Sun 11am–5.30pm	¥ ¥
		W
🚏		yayoikusamamuseum.jp
Ushigome-yanagicho		

Bic Camera
ビックカメラ

This chain camera and electronics store has everything you need for clicking and shooting.

1-11-1 Yurakucho, Chiyoda-ku

Yurakucho

Mon–Sun 10am–10pm

JP¥

¥ ¥

W

biccamera.co.jp

Photography buffs: you already know that the best gear comes from Japan. Names such as Nikon, Canon, FujiFilm, Olympus, Sigma, Sony … they're the pinnacle of the modern photography world, and they're all Japanese. While plenty of those brands have their own flagship stores here, it's even easier to step into Japan's photography megastore, Bic Camera.

    The Bic store in Yurakucho, near Ginza, is one of the largest, a nine-storey mega-mall selling a huge range of electronics and photography equipment. Here you'll find all of the digital camera bodies and lenses you could hope for, as well as tripods, memory cards, video equipment, drones, bags, maintenance gear and much more. The prices are competitive and the range second-to-none.

Toguri Museum of Art
戸栗美術館

The best of Japanese and other Asian ceramics is showcased in this impressive and extensive space.

1-11-3 Shoto, Shibuya-ku

Shibuya

Mon–Sun 10am–5pm

JP¥

¥

W

toguri-museum.or.jp

It's impossible to miss the passion Tokyo residents have for porcelain and other ceramics. Sit down to eat in any restaurant and the cup you drink from and the plate you eat off will have been chosen with the utmost care, and crafted with equal passion. Ceramics can elevate the dining experience and tell a story to the person eating.

It makes sense, therefore, that there's a museum dedicated to ceramics, in particular porcelain. Toguri Museum of Art is a neatly curated space featuring more than 7000 ceramic pieces in two of Japan's most famous styles, Imari and Nabeshima, as well as works from China, Vietnam and the Korean peninsula. You'll never look at your crockery in the same way again.

Pigment

Art lovers will find paints and inks in every colour imaginable at this beautiful Shinagawa store.

2-5-5 Higashishinagawa, Shinagawa-ku

Tennozu Isle

Tues–Wed 11.30am–7pm, Fri–Sun 11.30am–7pm

JP¥
¥ ¥

W
pigment.tokyo

There are all the colours of the rainbow – and many, many more: 4200 in total – on the walls at Pigment, an art store, laboratory and academy. This is nirvana for anyone with an interest in visual arts, from the pigments lining the walls, to the artisan-made calligraphy and paint brushes, and the papers, canvases, easels and other supplies.

The store offers workshops and courses, and is staffed by experts and patronised by obsessives. Pigment also serves as a museum, exhibiting rare and precious inkstones and brushes that showcase the history of art and design in Japanese culture. It's a pleasure just to explore and take in the beauty of Pigment's design, the work of architect Kengo Kuma.

Koncent

Homewares store keeps things local in design-friendly Kuramae, while stocking some amazingly useful goods.

2-6-10 Komagata, Taito-ku

Kuramae

Tues–Sun 11am–7pm

JP¥

¥

W

koncent.jp

There's a word in Japanese – zakka – that perfectly describes the sort of items you will find at Koncent: everyday pieces that improve your life; thoughtfully designed, highly functional 'things' that bring you joy. The perfect bottle opener is zakka. A humble coffee mug can be zakka.

And so, this large, all-white store stocks a huge range of knick-knacks and homewares designed in Japan, everything from cups and plates to vases, sponges, and little figurines that cling to the side of your cup noodles to hold the lid down. Koncent also has a third-wave coffee stand – operated by local purveyor Sol's – making it the perfect detour from a hard day of design scouring in the surrounding neighbourhood.

Kakimori

カキモリ

Custom-made notebooks and high-end fountain pens are the specialty at this stationery store.

1-6-2 Misuji, Taito-ku

Kuramae

Tues–Sun 11am–7pm

JP¥

¥¥

W

kakimori.com

The people of Japan care about stationery – writing paper, writing tools, wrapping paper and tape – in the same way they care deeply about the choice and design of anything that is passed from one person to another. So it's no surprise that the stationery available in Tokyo is both functional and beautiful. And Kakimori stocks some of the best.

This large, spacious store specialises in custom-made notebooks: you choose the type of paper, the front and back cover stocks, the type of binding, the type of fastener, and any words you want printed on the cover. Your notebook is then assembled on the spot. Kakimori also has a large range of fountain pens, pencils and biros.

Nakamichi-dori

中道通り

This bustling Kichijoji shopping street has a huge array of local design, craft and homewares stores to explore.

Kichijoji Honcho, Musashino-ku (Nakamichi-dori leads north-west from the train station)

Kichijoji

Various

JP¥

Various

This isn't a single store but rather an entire street filled with an almost uncountable number of local fashion and design boutiques, each worth calling into. There are coffee roasters here, electrical appliance dealers and even a Studio Ghibli museum; however, it's the unique design, homewares, stationery and fashion stores that are the reason to visit.

Check out Free Design for homewares from all of the top Scandinavian brands; find imported vintage goods at Wickie; browse local Japanese crafts at Markus; read a book and eat a curry at Cocktail Shobo; shop for leather goods at MIC; buy woollen yarns from Avril; pick up a beautiful antique at PukuPuku. There's also an enormous Uniqlo store at the beginning of the street.

Meals are Delightful

The ceramics here are beautiful, the space is lovely – and, yes,
the meals really are delightful.

You would visit this store just for the name – because meals absolutely are delightful, aren't they? However, meals are made even more delightful with the right crockery, and that's the true attraction of this Tomigaya store. Meals are Delightful is the flagship for Marumitsu Poterie Inc., a local ceramics brand that makes truly excellent tableware. The name refers to the cafe that's on the second floor; on ground level there's a showroom in which the company's works are displayed.

Marumitsu has two distinct brands: Studio M', which is everyday tableware often utilising traditional Japanese design; and Sobokai, a range of white porcelain crockery aimed more at the restaurant and hospitality industry. For the best experience at Meals are Delightful, head upstairs first for a bite to eat, choosing between simple fare such as muffins, fritters and European-style desserts, or going all out with a bento-style meal of Japanese delicacies. All of the food will be served on Marumitsu crockery, which means you can decide on the style that suits you best before wandering downstairs to pick up a few choice items.

1-17-5 Tomigaya,
Shibuya-ku

Thurs–Tues 11am–
6.30pm

JP¥
¥ ¥

W
marumitsu.jp

Yoyogi-Hachiman

Tokyo Skytree
東京スカイツリー

*One of Tokyo's most recognisable tourist attractions
has long queues, but amazing vistas.*

This is no ordinary tower: the Tokyo Skytree is the second tallest structure
in the world, behind only Dubai's Burj Khalifa; its top floor is 450 metres
above the ground, which is higher than the tip of the Empire State Building.
The views, as you could imagine, are spectacular – on a clear day here you
will be able to see all the way to Mount Fuji, not to mention across Tokyo
in its entirety.

The main problem with the Tokyo Skytree is the queues. This is
a popular attraction that's notorious for its long wait times, particularly
on weekends and holidays, and even more particularly when those days
happen to be sunny and clear. For foreign tourists there's a way around
this: by purchasing a 'Fast Skytree Ticket' from a dedicated counter at the
base of the tower. Even then, of course, you can wind up in a long queue of
foreigners, and you'll have to queue with everyone else at the top to get back
down. The best bet here is to show up early (it's open from 9am), and then
wander across to nearby Asakusa for some breakfast.

1-1-2 Oshiage, Sumida-ku   Mon–Sun 9am–9pm   JP¥ ¥¥

Tokyo Skytree   tokyo-skytree.jp

Tokyu Hands

急ハンズ渋谷店

You'll walk out of this eclectic store with enough to fill a suitcase – and maybe even the suitcase.

12-18 Udagawacho, Shibuya-ku

Shibuya

Mon–Sun 10am–9pm

JP¥

¥

W

tokyu-hands.co.jp

Everything you ever wanted – and plenty that you didn't, though you will likely buy anyway – can be found at Tokyu Hands. This sprawling Shibuya department store is an absolute treasure-trove of Japanese-made bits and bobs, gadgets and knick-knacks, all spread across a baffling array of 24 half-levels. It's the ultimate place for zakka, the everyday things that bring you joy, that have been crafted with such thought for perfection.

Tokyu Hands has the lot: travel accessories and luggage; a huge range of crockery and kitchen utensils; fitness equipment; stationery; art, design and craft supplies; miniature models; beds and linen; lights; and DIY woodworking materials ... You get the drift. Happy shopping.

Omotesando High Fashion

The leafy streets of Omotesando are lined with some of the world's most famous fashion houses.

Minamiaoyama

Omote-Sando

Various

JP¥

¥ ¥ ¥

Even if you're not buying, there's a distinct pleasure in window-shopping for some of the world's finest and most expensive garments in the swish district of Omotesando. Here you will find outlets for the likes of Comme des Garçons, Stella McCartney, Prada, Issey Miyake, Miu Miu, Balenciaga, Givenchy, Alexander McQueen, Burberry and more.

Each store is housed in an impressive work of modern architecture, each space designed by experts, each garment displayed at its best. The price tags on each of those garments might give you a heart attack, but hey, you're not here for bargains. You're here to marvel at the excess and appreciate the talent. And that's free.

The otaku have been unfairly maligned. Misunderstood, in many ways. The word otaku to so many people just means nerd or geek: someone who's into computer games and manga. Someone who's awkward and antisocial. Someone who dresses poorly and rarely goes out.

But that's not really what an otaku is. An otaku is just someone with obsessive interests who takes their particular subculture so seriously that their social life can suffer. Apply that definition and all of a sudden everyone in Tokyo, from artists to designers to musicians to cooks, could be described as an otaku.

For the purposes of this chapter, however, we're looking at manga and anime, at arcade games and their heroes, at kink and quirk – the likes of which you will only find in Tokyo. We're looking at the places that people who are into these subcultures hang out.

The heartlands for otaku culture are spread through Tokyo's north and east. They're in Akihabara, the electronics district that had its boom time in the '80s and '90s. They're in Nakano, with its manga superstores and its amazing array of collectables. And they're in Shibuya and Shinjuku, fashionable areas that still possess nerdy undercurrents. Whether you share the passions of the otaku or you would just like to understand their obsessions, this is a unique look into the soul of Tokyo.

44Sonic

アニソンBAR

This tiny, smoky bar caters to the manga and anime crowd with its figurines and themed drinks.

The stereotype of the socially awkward otaku might lead you to believe that these people won't exactly be out at bars drinking and carousing the night away. Except that's not true. 44Sonic is an anime lover's paradise, a small underground bar that's filled to bursting with figurines, comic books, movie posters, memorabilia, magazines and DVDs, designed for anime and manga fans to get together and share their passion over a few drinks.

Those drinks are something special too. The owner is an old-school anime fan who speaks English and who will happily design a cocktail based on your favourite fictional character. Be warned: there's a cover charge on top of your drink price. There's also sometimes karaoke, which you could take as a good or bad thing.

2-12-4 Asagayakita, Suginami-ku	Tues–Sun 7pm–12am	JP¥ ¥ ¥
Asagaya		W 44sonic.net

Otaku

Love Hotel Hill

Those who are shy and those who need privacy can take shelter in one of Tokyo's notorious love shacks.

So here's a thing: you have a hot date, and you think it might go well. But, you live at home with your parents. It's quite a small home, too, typical of Tokyo. It has thin walls. It has no privacy. What do you do? The answer is that you head to a 'love hotel', an establishment designed for those with kinky good times in mind, a provider of rooms that are available either for a 'rest' – up to four hours – or a 'stay', for the entire night. These places are everywhere in Tokyo, and you'll know when you've found one, thanks to the outlandish and often themed designs, the lack of windows, and the signs out the front announcing the rates.

Love hotels are very much an accepted part of Japanese culture now, nothing to titter over or frown upon. They're used by everyone from the socially awkward to the upwardly mobile, some of whom have hired their partners, and others who have met more organically. Travellers probably won't need to use a love hotel for its intended purpose. However, some of these places – particularly in Shibuya, on the famous Love Hotel Hill – are tourist attractions in their own right, themed establishments with riotous designs, including manga, Hello Kitty, and S&M torture chambers. Access is anonymous, via touchscreens at the door, and most rooms have all the mod-cons. Enter, and be dazzled.

Dogenzaka, Shibuya-ku   Various   JP¥
                                     ¥ ¥

Shibuya

Vending machines

You'll find anything and everything for sale at the touch of a button in Tokyo.

Various

JP¥

¥

Tokyo's vast army of vending machines seem like the perfect shopping opportunity for the socially awkward: there's no human interaction necessary. Simply put a few coins in the slot or swipe your public transport card, press a button and away you go.

The truth, however, is that vending machines are used by everyone, and they sell everything. You'll find drinks, both hot and cold, snacks, chocolates, even soups and sandwiches. Keep an eye out and you'll also pick up fresh fruit, an umbrella, popcorn, a Pokémon figurine, or a bottle of dashi.

It's generally frowned upon in Japan to have your drink on the go, so you'll see people standing by vending machines drinking their coffee before depositing the can in the bin provided.

Shiro-Hige's Cream Puff Factory

白髭のシュークリーム工房

One of Studio Ghibli's most famous characters comes in tasty, bite-sized form at this quaint bakery.

5-3-1 Daita, Setagaya-ku

Setagaya-Daita

Wed–Mon 10.30am–7pm

JP¥

¥

W

shiro-hige.com

Studio Ghibli's intense popularity means the animation house's museum (see p.185) is often booked out. You can, however, worship one of Ghibli's best-loved characters at Shiro-Hige's Cream Puff Factory, a small bakery in a storybook house that specialises in choux pastry in the shape of Totoro, the eponymous lead character in the anime film, *My Neighbor Totoro.*

Shiro-Hige's Totoro pastries are filled with sweet cream in a variety of flavours to match the season. Expect to find the likes of raspberry, peach, mango or chocolate inside. They're such kawaii (cute) little treats that you'll feel bad about biting into them – that is, until you taste them. The Totoros are take-away only; however, Shiro-Hige's Cream Puff Factory also has a small cafe on the second floor, called Tolo Coffee & Bakery.

Otaku

Studio Ghibli Museum
三鷹の森ジブリ美術館

The whimsical essence of the film studio behind Spirited Away
is captured at this popular museum.

For anime fans, this is the big one: an entire museum dedicated to the output of legendary filmmaker Hayao Miyazaki's Studio Ghibli. Most of Japan's highest-ever grossing anime films were produced by this cherished company: the likes of *Spirited Away*, *My Neighbor Totoro*, and *Ponyo*, all of which have earned an important place in Japanese culture as a whole.

The museum is set in Mitaka, hugging the edge of pretty Inokashira Park (see p.218), a short walk or bus ride from central Kichijoji. Its design will be immediately recognisable to fans of the studio's style of animation – a colourful, whimsical building filled with Ghibli characters and settings, made to make you feel like you're in the middle of a film. The studio's works are screened regularly at the museum, while there are also sketches and illustrations on display, plus interactive exhibits, a children's reading room, with books recommended by Miyazaki-san himself, a bookshop selling Ghibli favourites, and a cafe with outdoor seating overlooking the park. Tickets go on sale three months in advance, on the first day of each month, and can be purchased online from overseas via the JTB Group.

1-1-83 Shimorenjaku, Mitaka-ku

Kichijoji

Wed–Mon 10am–6pm

JP¥
¥ ¥

W
ghibli-museum.jp;
jtbgmt.com

Otaku

Mandarake

まんだらけ 中野店 買取処

From Transformers to toy trains, manga comics to baseball cards,
Mandarake has everything collectable.

Mandarake will blow your mind. Even if you're not into manga. Even if you have no interest in figurines or collectables. It will blow your mind.

This isn't just one store but a colossal 30 different shops all located in the Nakano Broadway mall – and all called Mandarake – each defined by the kind of niche items it carries. In some shops you will find wall after wall of manga comics, both new and used, both above board and a little on the icky side. In others you'll see figurines of manga and anime characters; in others, figurines from cult Hollywood films; in others still you will find vintage toys like Transformers, signed sports memorabilia, toy cars, baseball cards, J-pop collectables, model trains, posters, magazines, DVDs and more.

If it sounds intense, it is. Toy car shops play aggressive J-punk music. Otakus crowd into tight shop aisles looking for the perfect collectable. The stores don't seem to be laid out in any discernible order – you just poke your head in and see what's inside each one – and the sheer range of bits and pieces on offer is mind-boggling and impressive. You could spend hours here taking it all in, purchasing or just staring, and it would be time well spent.

5-52-15 Nakano,
Nakano-ku

Mon–Sun 12pm–8pm

JP¥
¥ ¥

W
mandarake.co.jp

Nakano

M's Pop Life
大人のデパート エムズ 秋葉原

Be titillated, turned on or grossed out
at this seven-storey sex shop.

There's a funny thing about Japan: it may appear to be quite a conservative
country, a community-minded place where no one strays too far from the
conventional. But there's another side that lurks not far below the surface,
a kinky side, an unashamedly sexual side that is right there if you care
to look for it.

One of those places you will find it is at M's Pop Life, thought to be
Japan's largest sex shop, a seven-storey behemoth packed with all of the
adult-oriented products you've ever imagined, and – it's safe to say – plenty
that you haven't. Each floor has a theme, ranging from DVDs to lingerie, and
costumes to sex toys.

In some ways it's all very normal. In other ways, definitely not. Much
like Japan itself.

1-15-13 Sotokanda,
Chiyoda-ku

Mon–Sun 10am–11pm

JP¥
¥

W
ms-online.co.jp

Akihabara

Otaku

GiGO Akihabara 3

秋葉原3号館

Shoot bad guys, dance to J-pop or dig for treasure
at this sprawling arcade parlour in Akihabara.

The rest of the world may have moved on from arcade parlours, taking their game-playing into their loungerooms and onto the internet. And Japan has done that too, without a doubt. Still, there is room in this gaming-obsessed nation for old-school arcade parlours to survive, and nowhere are they flourishing more strongly than in the suburb of Akihabara.

This is the home of three separate multi-level gaming centres that were once owned by Sega, but are these days branded as GiGO. Building three, known as 'GiGO Akihabara 3', is the best of them. The arcade is populated by a younger crowd who take their gaming seriously, twiddling joysticks and pulling out dance moves with intense concentration. They come to GiGO for the solid range of old-school video games, including plenty of driving games – keep an eye out for the four-player Mario Kart section – and first-person shooters, plus the dancing, taiko-drumming and lucky dip prizes that are eternally popular in Japan. On the top floor there's also a seriously high-tech virtual reality area in which you're given a backpack, a VR headset and a large gun and let loose on the baddies. Fun.

1-11-11 Sotokanda,
Chiyoda-ku

Mon–Sun 10am–11pm

JP¥

¥

W

tempo.gendasega.jp

Akihabara

Otaku

Radio Kaikan

秋葉原ラジオ会館

Legendary Akihabara mega-mall specialises in all things manga and anime.

1-15-16 Sotokanda, Chiyoda-ku

Akihabara

Various

JP¥

¥

W

akihabara-radiokaikan.co.jp

This is an entire shopping mall dedicated to manga, anime and personal electronics. It was established in 1957, relaunched after a major renovation in 2014, and continues to represent Japan's golden era of pop culture and gaming, a time when Goku and Astro Boy ruled the world.

There are 12 floors both above and below ground at Radio Kaikan jammed with different shops selling everything an otaku (or 12-year-old) could ever need, including models and figurines, trading and game cards, dolls and toys, hobby supplies, magazines, costumes, comics and more.

The mall has a few personal electronics and audio stores too, as well as a restaurant in the basement level and a convenience store on the first floor to keep shoppers fed and hydrated.

Pokémon Center Mega Tokyo

ポケモンセンターメガトウキョー ＆ ピカチュウスイーツ

Your one-stop shop for all things Pokémon – including Pokémon curry noodles.

3-1-2 Higashiikebukuro, Toshima-ku

Ikebukuro

Mon–Sun 10am–8pm

JP¥

¥

W

pokemon.co.jp

It feels like Pokémon was an anime wonder that boomed in the late '90s and then began to disappear. Only, Pokémon didn't disappear. The popularity of Pikachu, Mew, Charizard and co. continues to soar, thanks in part to the phenomenal success of Pokémon Go, though also in part to Japan's enduring love for classic characters.

Call past the Pokémon Center Mega Tokyo, something of a shrine to the game and its characters, as well as a shop. There are standard soft toys and figurines of Pikachu, plus plenty of limited-edition collectors' items, as well as Pokémon-themed tableware, stationery, slippers and nightgowns, candies, cookies ... and even Pokémon-branded curry noodles. There are a few arcade games to play, plus giant figurines to pose with.

Forget Melbourne and its small bars. Forget Barcelona and its tapas scene. Forget New York and its speakeasies, London and its pubs, Berlin and its clubs. Because the world's best city for drinking is Tokyo, hands down. This is a city that knows how to party, how to combine the best food with the best drinks, how to bring a sense of camaraderie and hospitality to the act of boozing, how to cater to absolutely everyone.

Tokyo is a huge city full of tiny bars, establishments that cater to only a few people at a time, staffed by passionate, knowledgeable bartenders who pour drinks and make conversation. There's just such a huge variety of venues: classy cocktail bars, raucous izakaya (local sake bars), cosy whisky bars, boozy karaoke joints, rocking metal bars, sophisticated snacking spots, wine bars, craft beer bars and so, so much more.

A night out drinking in the Japanese capital is a choose-your-own-adventure type of experience. Go big, go small, go boozy, go classy. It's up to you. Whatever you're into, whatever you feel like eating, drinking, listening to or talking about, you will find a bar in Tokyo that caters to it.

So 'kanpai', bottoms up, and enjoy.

Bar Yu-Nagi

銀座のバー 夕凪

The bartenders at this cosy Ginza cocktail joint use organic ingredients to create unique drinks.

6-8-6 Ginza, Chuo-ku

Ginza

Mon–Sat 6pm–2am

JP¥

¥ ¥

W

ggpw500.gorp.jp

You don't come to Yu-Nagi for the music – there often isn't any. You don't come for the wild party vibes – this is a quiet space where punters speak in hushed tones, focusing on the drinks in front of them. Yu-Nagi is all about cocktails that feature the finest organic fruits and vegetables from around Japan. Owner Toshiyuki Kamiki has a background in agriculture, and applies his passion for produce to his drinks.

Yu-Nagi is famous for its Bloody Marys, produced using the best tomatoes. The gin and tonic has organic lemon juice from the Hiroshima prefecture (famed for citrus), and a bourbon sour uses apple juice from Hirosaki. Yu-Nagi also stocks a range of blended whiskies, smooth drams in keeping with the calming vibe.

Uoshin
魚真 吉祥寺店

This classic izakaya serves up high-quality seafood dishes in a casual and friendly atmosphere.

2-18-8 Kichijoji Honcho, Musashino-ku

Kichijoji

Mon–Fri 5pm–12am, Sat–Sun 4pm–12am

JP¥

¥

W

uoshins.com

Izakaya (local sake bars) might just offer the most enjoyable style of dining in the world. These are typically casual, affordable little joints set up ostensibly for the consumption of beer and sake, though they also serve small plates of food that quickly become the main attraction. Izakaya are friendly and welcoming, and great places to meet locals.

Uoshin is a small chain of Tokyo izakaya that specialise in seafood, and for a place that offers its sake on an all-you-can-drink basis, there's some serious work that goes into its cuisine. The small plates range from sashimi to whole fried fish, grilled oysters and sushi rolls. The produce is fresh and the preparation expertly done. The venue is laidback and fun. And did I mention the all-you-can-drink sake?

Ginza Shimada

銀座 しまだ

The standing-bar concept is elevated to all new heights at this friendly, food-focused venue.

8-2-8 Ginza, Chuo-ku

Shinbashi

Mon–Sat 5–11pm

JP¥

¥ ¥ ¥

W

oreno.co.jp/restaurant/shimada

Traditionally, tachinomi (standing bars) are ultra-casual boozers where workers can call in for a quick beer and a cheap snack before heading home. There are no seats because no one has time for seats. These venues are usually a lot of fun, where you can slacken your tie and sip on a whisky high-ball as your day winds down.

Ginza Shimada, however, is not like that. Yes, it only fits 10 or so standing patrons, but the fit-out here is expensive, with a wooden bar and well-chosen art, the drinks are high-end – the carefully curated sake selection is top-notch – and the food is spectacular. We're talking kaiseki-style (multi-course) dishes like soba noodles dusted with smoky, umami-rich bottarga; prawn jelly topped with fresh sea urchin roe; Kyoto turnip simmered in dashi and served with grated daikon. Shimada is taking the concept of the tachinomi and elevating it to new heights. You'll want to go along for the ride.

Cafe Stay Happy

There's a huge dose of quirk at this cafe where beer and hammocks are the order of the day.

2-29-14 Daizawa, Setagaya-ku

Shimokitazawa

Wed–Mon 1–10pm

JP¥

¥¥

W

cafestayhappy.com

Here's a cafe that defies easy classification. Is it a flower-power hippie retreat for those who fancy lying in a hammock or curling up on a big pillow under a dreamcatcher? Is it a hardcore beer-lovers' bar that has one of the best selections of local and imported ales around? Or is it just a spot to grab some Western-influenced cafe food and watch the bustle of Shimokitazawa go by? The answer, somewhat bizarrely, is that Cafe Stay Happy is all of these things.

The two owners have travelled the world and speak great English, and will be only too happy to engage on passion points like travel, sustainability, capitalism and beer. This is a quirky and comfortable spot to sit and watch the world go by and reminisce about your backpacking days. And of course, to stay happy.

Shinjuku Golden Gai

新宿ゴールデン街

*Shinjuku's classic drinking district offers a whole range
of tiny bars to suit any taste or mood.*

If you love a dive bar then you're going to fall instantly for Golden Gai, an historic and ramshackle drinking area in the heart of Shinjuku. This is actually a full dive district, a scruffy network of narrow alleys lined with boozer after boozer in varying degrees of seediness, a place that probably should have been bulldozed years ago, but miraculously, thankfully, has been spared from gentrification's march. Most of the establishments in Golden Gai can fit no more patrons than you could count on your fingers; they're hyper-specialised, some with themes by music genre, others dedicated to photography, or sport, or with staff dressed in hospital gowns.

Plenty of bars in Golden Gai have a cover charge, so this isn't a place for a pub crawl, but rather one to pick an establishment that takes your fancy and settle in. Try Open Book (1-1-6 Kabukicho), a bar-cum-bookstore that specialises in lemon sours. Alternatively, settle in at Deathmatch In Hell (1-1-8 Kabukicho), a heavy metal bar that charges a fitting ¥666 cover. Or try Not Suspicious (1-1-7 Kabukicho), a quirky but friendly bar filled with handwritten notes left by former customers.

📍	🕐	JP¥
1-1 Kabukicho, Shinjuku-ku	Various	Various
🚃		
Shinjuku		

Mitsuya Saketen

三ツ矢酒店

*This old-school sake purveyor will help newcomers navigate
the murky world of Japanese rice wine.*

What sort of sake do you like? Dry or sweet? Filtered or cloudy? Aged in wooden barrels or stainless steel? Refined or rough? Do you prefer the soft, fragrant sakes of the Nagano prefecture, or the clean, dry sakes from Niigata?

Chances are, you will arrive in Japan not knowing the answers to any of these questions. And that's perfectly reasonable. The world of sake is a tough one for foreigners to negotiate. There are so many nuances to this cherished drink, as many as you would have with wine. The flavours and styles are regional, the techniques are varied, the quality ranges from the very cheap stuff served warm in izakaya (local sake bars) to the high-end drops that will set you back the cost of a night's accommodation for a bottle.

It's all fairly intimidating, which is where Mitsuya Saketen comes in. This venerable sake store in Nishi-Ogikubo has been around since 1926, and its staff are well versed in taking out the guesswork for inexperienced drinkers. Mitsuya stocks hundreds of sakes across a wide range of regions, styles and price points, and a chat to the personable experts here will help you decode the labels, as well as decide what style you like and which bottle is best for your price range. There will definitely be something to suit.

2-28-15 Nishiogiminami,
Suginami-ku

Nishi-Ogikubo

Mon–Sun
9.30am–9.30pm

JP¥
¥¥

W
sake-mituya.com/html

Rock Bar Mother

Get your metal horns in the air at this basement dive bar that lets drinkers choose the music.

1-11-1 Kabukicho, Shinjuku-ku

Shinjuku

Mon–Sun 7pm–5am

JP¥
¥

W
rockbarmother.jp

The good people of Tokyo love to rock in various ways, everything from the slicked-back hair of the 1950s greasers to the metal-horns-in-the-air head-banging of the modern punk and metal scene. Rock Bar Mother caters to the latter crowd with a wall of noise that will probably be off-putting to all but proper fans. You don't come here to chat, you come here to listen, because there's no other option.

Aside from the rock, one of the draws here is the friendliness of the staff, who will even let you choose the music, two songs for every drink purchased (though from the bar's song library, so no T-Swizzle). Choose carefully – the other punters are here to listen.

Zoetrope

There are more than 300 varieties of whisky to taste at this busy Shinjuku bar.

7-10-14 Nishishinjuku,
Shinjuku-ku

Seibu-Shinjuku

Mon–Sat 5pm–12am

JP¥

¥ ¥

The fame of Japanese whisky is beginning to spread, and dedicated single-malt drinkers around the world are as familiar with the likes of Yamazaki and Hakushu as they are Lagavulin and The Balvenie. Commercial whisky production began in Japan in 1924, when whisky obsessives Shinjiro Torii and Masataka Taketsuru set up the Yamazaki distillery on the outskirts of Kyoto. Today there are nine active whisky distilleries in Japan, which have been scooping up global awards.

All of this brings us to Zoetrope, a bar that's run by Atsushi Horigami, a man who's something of a whisky encyclopaedia, and who stocks more than 300 varieties of Japanese and imported drams. Describe what you like, and he'll find a whisky to fit your taste.

Niigata-Kan N'espace
新潟館ネスパス

Hugely popular prefectural antenna shop stocks an excellent range of Niigata sake, available to taste.

4-11-7 Jingumae, Shibuya-ku

Omote-Sando

Mon–Sun 10.30am–7.30pm

JP¥

¥

W

nico.or.jp

Plenty of Tokyo's antenna stores (see p.48) that sell produce and souvenirs from different prefectures around Japan proudly stock their local region's high-quality sakes; however, Niigata-Kan N'espace takes things a little further, with a great little bar offering tastings of a small, rotating selection of rice wines. It's especially good if you're unfamiliar with sake or can't read or speak Japanese.

The shop has three floors dedicated to the produce of Niigata, including a tourist information booth and two restaurants serving Niigata cuisine. If you're a fan of Japanese rice – and you should be, it's some of the best in the world – Niigata grows the best 'koshihikari' around, and a bag of it will make a handy souvenir for those with room to spare in the suitcase.

Ahiru Store

アヒルストア

Natural wine fans, rejoice: Ahiru Store in the heart of Tomigaya has all of your niche desires covered.

1-19-4 Tomigaya, Shibuya-ku

3-5454-2146

Yoyogi-Hachiman

Mon–Tues 6pm–12pm,
Thurs–Fri 6pm–12pm,
Sat 3–9pm

JP¥
¥¥

Ahiru Store is cool, and it knows it. Its owners know it. Its customers know it. The people lining up outside the bar hoping to become customers know it, too. This is perhaps Tokyo's best-known bar specialising in 'natural wine', a nebulous classification that attracts some hardcore vino fans.

Fortunately, Ahiru might be cool, but it's also cosy. It is a corner nook, a small room with a long wooden bar and a few barrels that act as tables for standing patrons. The food menu sticks to French bistro classics, the likes of pâté and tarte tatin. The service is friendly and the wine list, which features plenty of rare and sought-after producers from France and Italy, is always interesting.

Tsukinowaguma
ツキノワグマ

A rotating cast of local craft beers is featured at this cosy, friendly Gakugei joint.

2-20-4 Takaban, Meguro-ku

Gakugei-Daikagu

Mon–Sat 5pm–12am

JP¥

¥ ¥

Given Tokyo's love of all things niche and artisanal, it's a surprise that craft beer isn't more popular. In most bars you'll find only one beer on tap, generally, by a major brewery like Sapporo, Asahi or Kirin. Those are delicious too, which may explain the dearth of good microbreweries.

There are, however, a few bars keen to showcase the work of local artisans. One of those is Tsukinowaguma, set up by beer fanatic Megumi Fukuda in Gakugei-Daigaku. The bar is small and casual, just an elbow-shaped wooden counter and three beer taps, from which a rotating cast of artisanal IPAs, pale ales, göses, hefeweizens and more are poured. There are also bottles and cans of local brews.

Tofu Sorano

豆腐料理 空野（渋谷店）

A vegetarian-friendly izakaya that serves up tofu dishes in traditional, peaceful surrounds.

4-17 Sakuragaokacho, Shibuya-ku

Shibuya

Tues–Sun 5–11.30pm

JP¥

¥¥

W

foodgate.net

Vegetarians and vegans: I feel you. Tokyo is not a place that caters to you particularly well. Even the vegetable dishes in this city are often cooked with dashi, an essential Japanese stock that's made using dried fish. The solution? Tofu Sorano, a character-filled izakaya (local sake bar) in the back streets of Shibuya that does serve a few meat dishes, but focuses mainly on vegetarian- and vegan-friendly cuisine, most of which features the eponymous ingredient. Tofu here is treated with love and care, served fried, deep-fried, braised or steamed with complementary flavours and toppings. The dishes are served by friendly waitstaff in elegant, traditional surrounds, with low tables on tatami-mat floors. Regardless of your dietary preferences, you will love this little spot.

Cafe Arles

カフェアルル

Come for the coffee, stay for the cats: this quirky kissaten shows that nightlife doesn't have to be boozy.

Hanging out at a bar in Tokyo doesn't always mean getting drunk. Sometimes, you don't need alcohol at all. Cafe Arles, in the quiet backstreets of Shinjuku, is the ultimate expression of the fact that you can have an adult good time in the Japanese capital without slurring through a multi-lingual conversation with drunken salarymen. This place is an old-school kissaten, a coffee shop that's been around since the 1970s, and it doesn't look like much has changed since the doors were first flung open.

Arles is a small slice of mid-century France transported to Tokyo, a place of deep couches and European art prints, where jazz plays on the stereo and cigarette smoke wafts through the air. There's plenty of quirk to this place: two resident cats prowl the cafe floor and coffee is served with dried corn kernels and half a banana. If you don't mind the smoke though, this is the ideal place to hunker down with a book or a laptop and just soak up the arty, eclectic atmosphere.

5-10-8 Shinjuku, Shinjuku-ku

Mon–Sun 11.30am–10pm

Shinjuku-sanchome

3-3356-0003

JP¥
¥¥¥

Nature

Can the residents of one of the world's most populous urban areas really be obsessed with nature? Absolutely. And if you question that, just arrive in Tokyo around April, when the sakura (cherry blossoms) explode in a riot of colour and it seems like every resident of the city is outside to appreciate it, either photographing the flowers with an expensive camera, or sitting in a park with friends and admiring the spectacle during a traditional hanami (cherry blossom-viewing).

Even outside of cherry blossom season, Tokyo is a city that celebrates the natural world, particularly in autumn, when the changing leaves imbue the urban area with incredible colour. The city is dotted with parks and gardens, many of which are attractions in themselves, as beautifully designed as any work of art, and lovingly cared for. These green spaces offer the perfect respite from city life; they're calming, spacious spots ideal to wander in and relax, to sit and appreciate, to drink matcha tea and just enjoy the way the locals can curate nature and coax more beauty out of it than already exists.

Rikugien Gardens

六義園

Beautifully landscaped garden is designed to recreate scenes from famous poems.

6-16-3 Honkomagome,
Bunkyo-ku

Sugamo

Mon–Sun 9am–5pm

JP¥
¥

Rikugien is one of Tokyo's most beautiful gardens – in fact probably the most beautiful – and yet it's rarely visited, hidden as it is behind high walls in suburban Bunkyo-ku, an otherwise unremarkable part of the city. It's well worth the effort to find, however.

The park is actually a series of gardens that were built in the late 1600s, and designed to reflect the six elements of 'waka' poetry. Rikugien's hills, lawns, forests and ponds really do have a lyrical nature to them, and there are 88 scenes from famous poems recreated in nature here, for those with a sharp eye. The park also has several humble though beautiful teahouses – call into Fukiage Chaya to sip matcha and enjoy the view.

Meguro River

目黒川

Run-of-the-mill waterway becomes a major tourist attraction during spring.

Meguro-ku, between
Nakameguro and Meguro

Nakameguro

24 hours

JP¥
Free

For 11 months of the year this concrete canal is largely unremarkable, though it does provide a good running route for those who need some exercise. Come April, however, the sakura (cherry blossom) trees that line Meguro River – which is also known as Nakameguro Canal where it passes through that part of the city – explode with colour as the annual blossoms bloom. This is the time to see Meguro River in all its glory, though as you'd imagine it's very popular, and worth visiting early in the morning for the most peaceful experience, and the best chance to nail that perfect sakura photo.

Shinjuku Gyoen National Garden

新宿御苑

Escape from the bustle of the city into this peaceful and spacious parkland.

11 Naitomachi, Shinjuku-ku

Shinjuku

Tues–Sun 9am–6pm
(7pm in summer)

JP¥
¥

The contrast couldn't be more obvious: you walk from Shinjuku, which is Tokyo at its biggest and busiest, and into the Gyoen National Garden, where you're immediately at peace in nature. This is a park with a fascinating history, having once been a feudal lord's residence, then a recreation ground for the emperor's family, before being destroyed in World War II and later rebuilt as a public park.

Shinjuku Gyoen is one of the city's largest green spaces, with sprawling lawns, extensive walking paths, and manicured gardens dotted with bridges and ponds. It's also one of Tokyo's premier cherry-blossom-viewing spots, with more than 400 trees that bloom spectacularly.

Yoyogi Park

Popular urban green space attracts joggers, walkers, and even dancers.

2-1 Yoyogikamizonocho, Shibuya-ku

Harajuku

24 hours

JP¥

Free

This large park isn't just about natural beauty, but also culture: given its proximity to Shibuya and Harajuku, Yoyogi tends to attract a fashionable crowd, with plenty coming to see and be seen, including the 'greasers', the local group of '50s-style rockabilly dancers who strut their stuff in the park every Sunday.

That aside, Yoyogi is a large green space that's perfect for joggers and walkers, and which also has no shortage of attractive spots to sit in the shade and relax with a picnic from a nearby depachika (food hall). The park is known for its maple and ginkgo trees, which are spectacular in autumn, and provide perfect shelter during the warmer months.

Inokashira Park

都立井の頭恩賜公園

Take to the water at this pleasant park that doubles as a major hanami (cherry blossom-viewing) location.

1-18-31 Gotenyama, Musashino-ku

Kichijoji

24 hours

JP¥

Free

Set in Tokyo's western suburbs near bustling Kichijoji, Inokashira Park is mostly known for Inokashira Pond, a pleasant large body of water around which this lovely garden radiates. During the warmer months visitors can hire rowboats shaped like swans to take out on pond; the rest of the year it's just a nice feature to wander around on your way to the Studio Ghibli Museum (see p.185).

Inokashira is another of Tokyo's most popular hanami (cherry blossom-viewing) destinations, and if you arrive around early April you will find the place crowded and spectacular. It's also home to a shrine dedicated to Benzaitan, a goddess with a jealous streak, who supposedly curses love-struck couples as they walk past. Beware.

Todorokikeikoku Park

等々力渓谷公園 北側

Immersion in nature awaits at this lush, linear parkland in Tokyo's south-west.

1-22 Todoroki, Setagaya-ku

Todoroki

24 hours

JP¥

Free

It may seem as if Tokyo's urban sprawl is endless; however, it's relatively simple to swap the concrete jungle for real jungle. Todorokikeikoku Park is just a 20-minute train ride from Shibuya, but it's another world. A natural ravine has been converted into a recreational area, though one in which nature still runs wild in a pleasant contrast to the city's usually heavily landscaped parks and gardens.

Todorokikeikoku is a tranquil space where dense foliage surrounds a babbling brook, with a walking trail alongside that takes about half an hour to navigate. There's a Buddhist temple at one end, as well as access to Tamagawa-Tamagawa Park, another pleasant riverside space.

TOKYO SURVIVAL GUIDE

Tokyo is a friendly and largely very safe city – but it's also a nightmare if you don't know what you're doing. Follow these simple tips and you'll be fitting in and getting around in no time.

GETTING TO AND FROM TOKYO

Tokyo is serviced by two main airports, Haneda and Narita. To break things down to their simplest degree, think of them this way: Haneda good; Narita bad.

Haneda is close to downtown Tokyo, with excellent transport links, and is a high-quality modern airport with mind-blowingly good food options and an open-air observation deck. Narita is much further out, a bit of a nightmare to get around, and is serviced by a lot of budget airlines, as well as biggies such as ANA and JAL. Narita isn't a total disaster, but if you have the choice, go Haneda.

I could write an entire chapter on the transport options from each airport, though for best/fastest results from Haneda, use the Keikyu line to Shinagawa station to access the JR network. Take the Narita Express train from Narita to Tokyo station. Wherever you land or arrive, however, the best thing to do is pull out your phone with its spanking new data access (see below), plug your final destination into Google Maps (see p.222), and find all of the transport options laid out for you, with prices included.

GETTING AROUND TOKYO

Data

Tokyo can be extremely confusing even for those who've visited several times: it's a city of layers both above ground and underground, where you really have to think in 3D when you're trying to find your way around. Fortunately, there is help at hand, and it comes in the form of a mobile phone with data.

Buying a local SIM card is pretty much impossible for foreign visitors; however, you can either use your SIM from home, provided you have a reasonably priced global roaming package, or hire a SIM or portable wi-fi dongle from the airport on arrival in Tokyo. Both

The Essentials

TOKYO SURVIVAL GUIDE

Haneda and Narita airports have multiple shops that provide this service (haneda-airport.jp; narita-airport.jp).

Google Maps

This app, plus the data to use it, is your new best friend in this complicated beast of a metropolis. Even the system of addresses in Tokyo is a complete head-scratcher (see p. 17), and many bars and restaurants have no English signage. So, Google Maps to the rescue. Simply plug the name of the shop, bar or restaurant you're trying to find and follow the app's instructions (and the blue dot). For using public transport, enter your train station, and the app will tell you which train to catch, which platform to use, where on the train to ride for best access to the next station, which exit to take, and more. Best. Friend.

IC card

Your key to Tokyo's vast public transport system is an IC card, a prepaid swipe card that will get you onto the subway, trains, buses, trams and more. This is particularly handy given Tokyo's public transport is handled by multiple companies and you'll need to switch between them, often on a single journey – an IC card means you just swipe and go.

There are two main IC cards sold at ticket machines at most train and subway stations: Pasmo,

sold by Tokyo Metro, and Suica, sold by JR. Both will give you access to all transport options, and can also be used at most vending machines and even a lot of restaurants within the stations. No ID is required for purchase, simply pay and you're away.

LOCAL KNOWLEDGE

Book ahead

Plenty of the city's best attractions – and almost all of its high-end restaurants – require bookings weeks in advance. The best way to make izakaya (local sake bars) and restaurant bookings, given English speakers in Tokyo are still rare (making phone bookings difficult), is to use TableAll (see p.45), or, if you're staying in a hotel, ask the concierge to make the bookings for you by phone. Accommodation (see p.228) should be booked well in advance, too.

Restaurants

Dining out in Tokyo is one of life's truly great pleasures, but it can also be something of a challenge. Where do you eat? What do you eat? How do you order?

The good news is that most Tokyo restaurants, unless they're particularly high-end or particularly popular, work on a first-in, first-served basis. This is particularly true of the surprisingly high-quality eateries that you will find on the top two levels (and sometimes basement levels) of large department stores and train stations.

The ordering process varies: ramen bars usually have ticket machines that you'll use before sitting down, and hand your order over to the chef. At other restaurants, waitstaff will take your order as usual. At the truly high-end places, food will be served omakase (chef's choice).

Cafes

There are three types of cafes in Tokyo, a city that loves coffee but isn't always sure how to drink it. There are the 'third-wave' cafes that serve modern, Italian-style espresso (some of which you'll find in the Nyuu-Ebu chapter, see p.97). There are the second-wave American chains that pump out grande-mocha-latte concoctions with a flavouring shot of your choice. And then there are kissaten, the original Tokyo cafes, often dark, smoky joints where coffee is served simply black or white and slid across the bar in china cups, places where people gather to chat or read or just simply be.

Opening hours

Although Tokyo is a 24-hour city, its citizens tend to eat quite early, so you'll want to follow suit – plan to sit down to lunch before 1pm, and dinner well before 8pm. For late-night eats, try ramen bars or izakaya (local sake bars), which tend to stay open until around 11pm or midnight.

If you like to sleep in, Tokyo is the city for you. There's not much that happens before about 11am: most shops won't open until then, and there's also not much of a breakfast or brunch culture here.

Cash

Though an increasing number of shops and restaurants in Japan now accept credit cards, particularly since COVID, this is still a largely cash-based society – even some high-end eateries only accept large wads of cash – so stock up. Japan-based banks don't accept foreign cards, but the cash machines (ATMs) at all 7-Elevens and post offices do (and they're everywhere).

Safety

Tokyo is one of the safest cities in the world – the safest, according to some metrics. Still, that doesn't mean you're in no danger whatsoever. The best bet is to trust your judgement. If a situation feels uncomfortable to you, then it's time to back out. Be polite and walk away from whatever situation you're in. Know where the nearest subway station is and jump on a train. Or simply blend into the crowd.

Religion

There's a deep spirituality to Tokyo, and indeed all of Japan, that isn't always obvious in the glare of the big-city lights. But like so much of the Japanese identity, it lurks

The Essentials

just below the surface, integral and devoutly observed. There are two main religions in Japan, Buddhism and Shintoism. Buddhism is an imported set of beliefs, which arrived in the country around the 6th century CE, whereas Shintoism is an indigenous faith unique to Japan. You will see monuments dedicated to both of these religions – temples for Buddhism, shrines for Shintoism – throughout Tokyo, from the grandest of temples to the tiniest neighbourhood shrines.

ETIQUETTE GUIDE

Don't be one of 'those' tourists. Follow these simple steps and you'll avoid giving offence or annoying anyone (well, mostly).

Business cards
It doesn't matter if you're in the country for work or pleasure: the exchange of business cards – called meishi – is an important transaction in Japan, a way of demonstrating your interest in another person and respecting their position and career. Always carry yours, and receive other people's with two hands, reading it carefully before storing it in a case.

Eating
No one eats on the go in Japan. You don't eat a take-away burger or drink a coffee while you stroll. Consume your food and drink in the place you bought it. Even if you're eating street food or from a vending machine, stand still or find somewhere to sit.

Blowing your nose
It's considered pretty bad form to blow your nose in public in Japan. Go to a bathroom – they're all spotlessly clean. Even sniffling is considered more acceptable than nose-blowing.

Dressing well
Japanese people, especially in the larger cities, dress extremely well. They dress formally for work, and stylishly for play. If you want to fit in and show respect for your hosts, put some thought into your outfits, and avoid specialist travel gear (unless you're out hiking).

Tipping
One of the true glories of travel in Japan is that you just don't tip. At all. Don't even leave your change on the table – someone will run after you to give it back.

Shoes & slippers
When entering someone's home, remove your shoes. In some restaurants people take off their shoes (you'll see them neatly lined up in racks by the door), and also inside temples. In some homes and guesthouses slippers are provided to use when you're indoors, and separate slippers will

be offered to visit the bathroom. Use them.

Bowing

If feels a little awkward at first, but if you want to greet Japanese people in the way they're accustomed, then you need to bow. Don't worry too much about the exact etiquette – locals will cut you plenty of slack. Just tilt forward at the waist, with arms by your sides, and you're all set. If that still feels too weird, simply nodding hello will do the job.

Tattoos

Tattoos in Japan are still associated with the Yakuza organised-crime group, and tend to make locals feel uncomfortable. If you're all tatted up, try to wear trousers and long sleeves. You'll also have to do your research before visiting an onsen – most don't allow entry to anyone with ink.

Chopsticks

Any time you're presented with wooden chopsticks at a restaurant, it's considered rude to snap them apart and then rub them together – the suggestion being that the chopsticks are of poor quality. Just lay them on their rest. Don't wave them around or point with them either. Chopsticks are only for eating.

Queuing

Tokyo is no place to be pushing in with elbows out when queuing.

Japanese people are fastidious queuers who will wait patiently in line to board a train, or to buy a coffee, or to do pretty much anything, really. Take your place and shuffle forward.

Signage

Take a look around – there are always signs telling you what to do and signs telling you what not to do. If you're in any doubt about where you're going or how you should be behaving, have a quick scan for a sign and heed its advice.

Phones

Mobile phone etiquette in Japan is very similar to eating etiquette. Don't talk on the phone when you're on public transport or on the street. Go somewhere out of the way to make your call, then move on.

Rubbish

You'll notice that there are almost no public rubbish bins in Japan. Vending machines will usually have a small receptacle for recyclable cans, but that's it. The idea is that you'll carry your rubbish with you and dispose of it at your home or accommodation.

Pouring drinks

Should you find yourself out drinking with new Japanese friends, bear in mind it's bad form to pour your own drink from a communal vessel. Always pour others' and wait for

The Essentials

someone to top your drinks up. Also, don't eat straight from communal dishes. Place food on your own plate before eating it, and reach for it using the top of your chopsticks; i.e. the ends that won't go into your mouth.

Wearing your yukata

Plenty of guesthouses and ryokans (traditional, boutique hotels) in Tokyo will supply a yukata, a light, casual robe to be worn as you grab a beer from the in-house vending machine or go to the breakfast room. Unless you're staying in an upmarket hotel chain, this will be fine. Just ensure you wear the yukata properly, wrapping the left side over the right, and tying it tightly with the sash.

Onsen rules

Japan is world famous for its bathhouse, or onsen culture, and yet visitors to Tokyo are often disappointed by the lack of facilities to try. There are several reasons for this: onsen culture is closely linked with appreciation for the natural world, which is why people tend to head out to the countryside to visit an onsen; it's also closely linked to the availability of warm, mineral-rich springwater, of which the Tokyo area doesn't have a huge amount. Onsens aren't a big part of Tokyo life, which is why I haven't dedicated an entire section to the etiquette required, although see

Tiyo no Yu (see p.70) for some tips. If you do decide to go to a public bathhouse, you should research the correct etiquette before visiting. The unwritten rules here are complex and always adhered to.

Observing

If in doubt in Tokyo – and you will be in doubt – in any situation, just look around and see what everyone else is doing. Copy them. Japanese people don't expect you to know everything, and they're usually very accommodating with foreigners. Make an effort, and you will be welcomed.

GUIDE TO EATING SUSHI

Style & price

Sushi restaurants in Tokyo vary wildly in terms of quality and cost. There are generally three levels of sushi experience.

The lowest (cheapest) and the one in which you'll have to worry the least about obeying the following rules is kaiten sushi (conveyor belt sushi). This is the same as your standard sushi train back home. Some of these in Tokyo work on an all-you-can-eat basis, and they're usually bustling and friendly.

Next up you have the casual a-la-carte sushi restaurants. At these you'll either sit at a bar in front of the itamae (chef), or at a table nearby. You'll be able to order

The Essentials

okimari, a set course of between 6 and 15 pieces of nigiri and rolled sushi, which will all be served together. You'll often find these sorts of restaurants on the top levels of department stores or in train stations.

The last version is the luxury or high-end sushi restaurant, where the atmosphere is quiet and reverent, and the bill is usually astronomical. Guests sit at a wooden bar in front of the chef, who often chats as they work. There's usually no menu and no prices advertised – everything fluctuates daily, depending on what the chef can find at the market. Ordering is omakase (chef's choice), so you just sit back and wait as anywhere between 15 and 30 pieces of sushi are made in front of you and handed over one by one. This is the ultimate sushi experience, but very pricey. Book well in advance. These places usually only seat about 10 people, and they're very popular. The chefs also like to know in advance about any dietary requirements.

Sushi etiquette

Sushi chefs are very particular about no perfumes or strong fragrances, the thinking being that the smell of perfume will affect the taste of some very expensive fish. This goes for both men and women.

The wooden bar you sit at in a high-end sushi restaurant is usually made of Hinoki cypress, a beautiful timber that is quite soft, and marks easily. Remove your watch and don't rest your phone on it or anything else that could scratch it.

It can be a surprise to find that a lot of shop and restaurant owners don't like having their wares photographed. That goes especially for sushi chefs. Get the OK before snapping.

Sushi restaurants are designed to be social. This isn't a place for loud, boozy conversation; however, do feel free to chat to the itamae (chef) behind the counter. But don't ask for their recommendation of what's good. It's all good.

Sushi is all about the rice. Yes, the fish has to be well sourced and fresh, but sushi chefs truly pride themselves on their rice, which has to be good quality, cooked properly and served at the perfect temperature, which means that as soon as a piece of sushi is plonked down in front of you, you should eat it. *Go*. You have about 30 seconds before the chef will start to become annoyed.

In a high-end sushi restaurant, the fish will often be seasoned for you, with a tare (sauce) that the chef applies as they see fit. In other sushi joints, you'll have to season your own fish, which means dipping it in soy sauce. However, the idea here is to go easy, and only dip the fish into the sauce, not the rice.

In any restaurant in Japan, sushi or otherwise, it's very bad form to order more food than you can eat. Make sure you finish whatever is in front of you.

The more casual sushi joints are designed to get customers in and out relatively quickly, so once you're finished eating, don't hang around for a chat.

ACCOMMODATION GUIDE

One of the great things about Tokyo is the sheer breadth of accommodation, including several unique options, all of which are generally safe, reliable, fastidiously cleaned, and worth giving a try.

If you're staying in Tokyo for more than a few days, split your accommodation between two major areas on opposite sides of the city – it will make a huge difference to your enjoyment of the city and it will mean you spend less time on public transport. For example, spend a few nights in Asakusa in the east, exploring Kuramae, Nihonbashi and Ginza; then, move to Shibuya, in the west, to see the likes of Shinjuku, Ebisu, Shimokitazawa and Koenji.

Hotel
Japanese hotels work in the same way as Western hotels, though there are a few different tiers available in Tokyo. These range from luxurious, high-end properties with all the mod-cons, to the more basic 'business hotels', to traditional Japanese properties that often have tatami-mat floors and futon beds.

Hostel
Tokyo has a wide range of hostel accommodation that's usually clean, friendly and well run. This is a great option for anyone travelling on a budget, as this can be an expensive city, particularly if you want to base yourself in a popular area.

Ryokan
A ryokan is a traditional and often very beautiful boutique hotel that usually features an immaculate garden and a bathhouse onsite. Rooms are simple and elegant, with tatami-mat floors, paper walls, futon beds and a small table and chairs, and guests are provided with a sumptuous dinner and breakfast. This is a must-do experience if you can afford it.

Minshuku
For those who can't afford the pricey ryokans, minshukus are Japanese-style bed and breakfasts. Minshukus are usually family-run affairs, where guests sleep in small, simple rooms on tatami-mat floors, and enjoy home-style but still quite elaborate meals in shared dining rooms. There are plenty of these in Tokyo's outer suburbs.

The Essentials

TOKYO SURVIVAL GUIDE

Airbnb

Though there's been something of a crack-down on apartment rentals in Tokyo, with strict licensing laws, there are still plenty of homes available for rent through Airbnb and similar home-sharing websites. It can be a great window into local Japanese life or to immerse yourself in a normal neighbourhood.

Love hotel

Stick with me here. It may seem as if a love hotel (see p.181) would be a pretty tacky place to spend a night, but this is a genuine option for someone looking for a bed. The rooms at love hotels tend to be quite spacious by Tokyo standards, plus they have all the mod-cons, and work on a walk-up basis. And if you find yourself in that awkward period between your flight's arrival and check-in time at your hotel, you can rent a room here in four-hourly blocks.

Capsule hotel

Travelling on the cheap? Have no problems with claustrophobia? Japan is famous for its ultra-small capsule accommodation, where travellers sleep in tiny pods that have no more than a curtain for privacy. Onsite vending machines sell cheap snacks and drinks, and there are shared bathing facilities. It's an experience, if nothing else.

Onsen resort

Admittedly, this is something you'll find more in the country areas than in Tokyo. The capital city does, however, have plenty of hotels that have bathhouses on site, which form a big part of the experience. Entry to these facilities is included in the room rate, and is unlimited. Be warned, however: you'll be expected to go completely naked in shared (though gender-specific) facilities, and travellers with tattoos may be denied entry.

Manga cafe

Though these cafes, usually found in tech-centric neighbourhoods such as Shinjuku and Akihabara, are ostensibly there to sell comics and provide spaces for customers to read said comics, they also have private rooms, with couches and computers, that can be rented in 24-hour blocks, providing cheap – if not exactly luxurious – lodgings for adventurous travellers.

PHOTO CREDITS

All photos © Ben Groundwater,
except:
Yulia Skogoreva: p.26, p.64, p.72,
p.84, p.96, p.100, p.104, p.108, p.116,
p.118, p.120, p.126, p.134, p.146,
p.157, p.158, p.166, p.179, p.184,
p.188, p.190, p.192, p.202, p.204,
p.205, p.208, p.209;
Alamy: p.ii, p.vi, p.2, p.5, p.10, p.66,
p.77, p.102, p.140, p.142, p.142, p.155,
p.180, p.194;
Shutterstock: p.79, p.81 , p.86, p.88,
p.90, p.93, p.128, p.159, p.164, p.165,
p.172, p.200, p.212, p.215, p.216,
p.217, p.218, p.219;
Tanukiphoto: p.147;
Table All: p.44;
Unsplash: p.ii Banter Snaps, p.vi
Ryoji Iwata, p.2 Claudio Guglieri, p.5
Chatnarin Pramnapan, p.10 Azlan
Baharudin, p.220 Liam Burnett Blue;
p.226 Gabriel Forsberg.

The Essentials

ARLING & HONEY

ry!

Hi-cherry has become more cute and powerful!!!
Photogenic Hi-cherry. That has completely renewable.

THANKS

It's impossible to have both a family and a career – particularly a career in travel – without someone else making a sacrifice and being there to do the hard work, and that person in my life is my amazing partner Jess. Thank you, Jess, for being my 'wife', for being there when I'm not, for being an incredible mother to our children and for doing all the truly vital work while I'm off reviewing izakaya, or whatever it is I claim to do. This book wouldn't have happened without you; our family and our lives together wouldn't happen without you.

I would also like to thank the wonderful team at Hardie Grant Travel, including Melissa Kayser and Megan Cuthbert, for having the faith in me to complete this project, for their support throughout, and for going along with a few of my weirder ideas. I owe plenty of gratitude, too, to my editor Alice Barker, who is responsible for the shiny, polished copy you see in front of you. I'm also indebted to Yulia Skogoreva, whose beautiful images adorn some of the pages of this book. A huge thank you, as well, to Lila Theodoros, the designer of this book, and Rosanna Dutson for poring over the copy.

And finally, I want to send out a huge thanks to the kind, generous, welcoming, funny, and occasionally boozy people of Tokyo. I've learned so much about this city and experienced so many of its fascinating quirks and eccentricities, thanks to chance encounters with helpful strangers. To those countless people: arigato gozaimashita.

Published in 2022 by Hardie Grant Explore,
an imprint of Hardie Grant Publishing

Hardie Grant Explore (Melbourne)
Wurundjeri Country
Building 1, 658 Church Street
Richmond, Victoria 3121

Hardie Grant Explore (Sydney)
Gadigal Country
Level 7, 45 Jones Street
Ultimo, NSW 2007

www.hardiegrant.com/au/explore

Hardie Grant acknowledges the Traditional
Owners of the Country on which we work, the
Wurundjeri People of the Kulin Nation and the
Gadigal People of the Eora Nation, and recognises
their continuing connection to the land, waters
and culture. We pay our respects to their Elders
past and present.

Maps in this publication contain data sourced from
the following organisations:

© OpenStreetMap contributors - OpenStreetMap
is made available under the Open Data
Commons Open Database License (ODbL) by
the OpenStreetMap Foundation (OSMF): http://
opendatacommons.org/licenses/odbl/1.0/. Any
rights in individual contents of the database are
licensed under the Database Contents License:
HYPERLINK "http://opendatacommons.org/
licenses/dbcl/1.0/" http://opendatacommons.org/
licenses/dbcl/1.0/

Data extracts via Geofabrik GmbH HYPERLINK
"https://aus01.safelinks.protection.outlook.
com/?url=https%3A%2F%2Fwww.geofabrik.
de&data=02%7C01%7Cemilymaffei%40
hardiegrant.com%7Cd0cde0c345d4c0
8ae4608d7c08f346a%7Cbd986eca22fd45
03bb75fd21d880c7e7%7C0%7C0%7C6
37189593595538317&sdata=GHotW8kpN2P6
pJhfSveoD7yaPXYgg2n0BKNXfiZlAPQ%3D&
reserved=0" https://www.geofabrik.de

Neon Lights in Tokyo
ISBN 9781741177015

10 9 8 7 6 5 4 3 2 1

Publisher
Melissa Kayser
Project editor
Megan Cuthbert
Editor
Alice Barker
Proofreader
Rosanna Dutson
Kanji consultant
Nyree Jacobs
Cartographer
Claire Johnston
Design
Muse Muse
Production coordinator
Simone Wall

Printed and bound in China by LEO Paper
Products LTD.

The paper this book is printed on is certified
against the Forest Stewardship Council®
Standards and other sources. FSC® promotes
environmentally responsible, socially beneficial
and economically viable management of the
world's forests.

A catalogue record for this
Book is available from the
National Library of Australia